CROSSCURRENTS *Modern Critiques*

CROSSCURRENTS *Modern Critiques*

Harry T. Moore, *General Editor*

Andor Gomme

Attitudes to Criticism

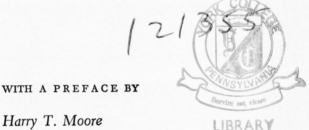

WITH A PREFACE BY

Harry T. Moore

Carbondale and Edwardsville

SOUTHERN ILLINOIS UNIVERSITY PRESS

To my mother

PREFACE

LITERARY CRITICISM was once only a part-time activity. The earliest critics, such as Plato and Aristotle, dealt with it only among many intellectual exercises. And, across the ages, criticism remained an incidental or secondary function. In the eighteenth century, for example, Dr. Johnson was a great critic, but many other things as well; in the nineteenth, Matthew Arnold, however we may rate his work now, was principally a poet and only afterward a critic. But in our own age, criticism has become a full-time writing occupation, even when the writer practicing it belongs to a special group. Examples of men who devote themselves entirely to criticism are too numerous to need mention here.

Andor Gomme, author of this book, is one of the many in all countries who write literary criticism from an academic base. He teaches at Keele University, which was the first of the newer group of English institutions to begin operations after the Second World War; Keele dates from 1949. Mr. Gomme, who has also taught in the United States, has distinguished himself as a critic and reviewer. In the present volume he undertakes an examination of various critical theories: the intention of his study, he says, "is not to add yet another to the welter of critical theories generally available, but to express a particular view of a number of those that already exist."

In examining the work of various authors, Mr. Gomme deals at length with John Crowe Ransom, Kenneth Burke, Yvor Winters, and F. R. Leavis. He is stringently critical of all of them except Leavis, a man whom some people can't read, not because he is obscure but because he is usually in a rage—this is the reason given by that master critic, Edmund Wilson, for not reading Leavis. But Mr. Gomme can read him, and makes some illuminating comments about his work, notably the earlier books. Mr. Gomme particularly values Leavis for his avoidance of general theorizing, and for his practice of dealing concretely with the poetry or fiction under immediate consideration.

Mr. Gomme has a higher regard for the other critics he investigates than appears in most of his statements about them; but in emphasizing points of disagreement he often illuminates their work while indicating his own method of approach. Actually, he has no definite method, nothing so rigorous as a system, for he consistently demonstrates that he believes that theory should not direct criticism. In the case of Ransom, he shows how wrong that critic is in attempting to exclude subjective and human elements (which in any event Ransom doesn't always succeed in doing). Mr. Gomme treats Kenneth Burke chiefly in his relation to his earlier work, which is somewhat Marxian and is more comprehensible than his later writings. (Mr. Gomme is quietly amusing when he takes up such aspects of Burke as his statement about Mark Twain and chain stores.) Yvor Winters, who pronounces against didacticism, is shown to be didactic in that the evaluations he insists are the heart of criticism are essentially didactic because they are rigorously moral evaluations. Throughout, Mr. Gomme deals with his material in terms of the question of relevance: which elements are the proper ones to use in judging literature?

This is a book which will probably find many readers in this age of criticism and of the criticism of criticism, for it is a book that is, in the truest sense of the word, challenging. Those who discover it will proclaim their discovery, in attitudes ranging from indignation to happy agreement. It will leave no one unmoved. Turn the page and see for yourself.

HARRY T. MOORE

Southern Illinois University
August 12, 1965

Contents

Criticism . . . must always profess an end in view, which, roughly speaking, appears to be the elucidation of works of art and the correction of taste. The critic's task, therefore, appears to be quite clearly cut out for him; and it ought to be comparatively easy to decide whether he performs it satisfactorily, and in general, what kinds of criticism are useful and what are otiose. But on giving the matter a little attention, we perceive that criticism, far from being a simple and orderly field of beneficent activity, from which impostors can readily be ejected, is no better than a Sunday park of contending and contentious orators, who have not even arrived at the articulation of their differences. Here, one would suppose, was a place for quiet co-operative labour. The critic, one would suppose, if he is to justify his existence, should endeavour to discipline his personal prejudices and cranks—tares to which we are all subject—and compose his differences with as many of his fellows as possible, in the common pursuit of true judgment. When we find that quite the contrary prevails, we begin to suspect that the critic owes his livelihood to the violence and extremity of his opposition to other critics, or else to some trifling oddities of his own with which he contrives to season the opinions which men already hold, and which out of vanity or sloth they prefer to maintain. We are tempted to expel the lot.

These words, from one of T. S. Eliot's most distinguished essays,[1] may well occur to anyone now contemplating the critical scene: they seem as true and as relevant today as when they were written over forty years ago. The aim of the present book is not to add yet another to the welter of critical theories generally available, but to express a particular view of a number of those that already exist. It will have served its purpose if it has helped to reduce contentiousness by articulating certain differences, and at the same time stating as unambiguously as possible a reasonably consistent view of the parties and ideas involved. It would be an impertinence in an outsider to attempt to *compose* these differences: that is for the critics themselves if they are minded to it. What I seek to do is to draw out and display certain attitudes to criticism: I hope that I have not done this in a partisan spirit, but I have not pretended to be innocent of attitudes in myself. Among those referred to in my title I am conscious of the working of my own. It would be idle to try to eliminate personal preferences and convictions from one's writing on such a topic. By being as clear-spoken as possible, I hope to have given the reader the chance to take his own bearings on my opinions.

The order of the four principal chapters in the book is governed by a special interest in the problem of *relevance:* what factors may one properly bring into the judgment of a work of art? The critics whose work is examined in some detail have been chosen as representing a wide range of fairly distinct views on this issue. And my essay moves from what I should call a position of minimum relevance—one in which art is kept strictly within an aesthetic framework and criticism forbidden to take its criteria from outside—to one which includes perhaps as much as is possible of the critic and of the whole society in which he lives. It meets on the way several sectional interests, all of which, I suggest, restrict or distort the value and capacity of both art and criticism.

I must stress that the essay is in no sense a survey of critical theories; it is not even a survey of the work of the four men whose work I chiefly consider. They have been chosen as representing clearly points of view of enough importance and contrast to prompt many of the characteristic questions which arise in any discussion of the function and methods of criticism; and it is the points of view in which I have been primarily interested. My texts have been chosen accordingly, and I hope that the resulting picture is not unduly inaccurate—it certainly is not full. Readers will find that it is Ransom's *theories* that I have concerned myself with, and not the various essays in criticism which so often seem to bear scant relation to the theory. Again I have not considered the more recent "neo-liberal" writings of Kenneth Burke, not just because of their enormous difficulty but because, in his earlier, Marxist, period Burke exercised his considerable energies and intelligence in a direction of great interest and potential danger for literature. It is naturally among Marxists that the endeavour to give a political *direction* to literature is most clearly and consistently upheld; but the only essential factor in determining my choice was that Burke shows so well how a set of political attitudes can determine a critic's "methodology" and hence the character of his critical activity.

It is in the chapter on Yvor Winters that I am most keenly aware of the deficiencies in my account. This chapter represents a decidedly partial view of the work of a remarkably gifted critic. For particular reasons of my own I have concentrated on aspects of Winters' work with which I often strongly disagree; but such has been this work's usual reception that I should not like my own criticism of it to appear without recording my feeling that among it is to be found some of the most perceptive, most intelligent, and most telling writing about literature to be done this century. Extremely valuable observations and correctives are to be found everywhere; and I believe that most open-minded readers have found themselves stimulated to a more accurate and explicit definition of their own viewpoints by essays of Winters' with which, in the main, they profoundly disagree. But there are, too, essays which, in a world that recognized serious and coherent standards, would rank as classics: for example, those on James, on Poe, on Frost and (I think) on Yeats. Winters' individualism can have unfortunate results; but it is unquestionably the attitude of a man who thinks deeply for himself.

In this chapter and in my fourth, my discussion is more largely in terms of criticism than of critical theory. In Winters' case, his criticism keeps his frequently set-out theoretical position so constantly in view that it is very easy to see the day-to-day working of his principles. Leavis is alone among the critics I have chosen in having done next to no explicit theorizing on criticism, so that his presuppositions must be discussed almost entirely through his practical work. This may raise a doubt about the propriety of closing my study with the work of a man whose principles are always seen "in solution." To this I think there are two answers. In the first place, while it is easier to attack an explicit theory than one only to be seen when it is thoroughly worked into a body of critical work, it is also easier to defend it—at least in the semi-philosophical manner favoured by most of the writers I consider. Secondly, I hold it a mark of a true sense of critical tact and relevance that theory (if it is to be made explicit at all) should be a construct out of practice, in which case it is quite likely that a general position can hardly even be convincingly made out apart from the particular judgments which give it substance.

I offer here my thanks to a number of friends whose interest and help have been unsparingly given. Dr. Theodore Redpath worked hard on the manuscript in its early stages; Mr. Geoffrey Strickland and Mr. Richard Gooder have each read part of later versions, and the criticism of all three has much improved the book. The encouragement of Professor L. C. Knights, Mrs. Rosemary Zeeman, and others has helped me over more than one dark period. And to two people I owe more than I know how to gauge: to my wife for the grace and steadiness of her constant good humour and good sense, and for her unfailing readiness to put aside whatever she was doing when I asked for her help; and to Dr. F. R. Leavis, who has always been so willing to give of his time and energy, and the influence of whose work and personal example is beyond calculation.

ANDOR GOMME

Keele
November, 1964

Attitudes to Criticism

1 THE POSSIBILITY
OF RELEVANCE

AMONG THEORIES about the nature of art, a possible division is between those that are preoccupied with the *effects* of a work of art on its actual or potential audience and those that seek to establish art as an autonomous realm marked out by one or more, quite distinct, defining properties. This division is not necessarily exhaustive, and the two categories may even overlap; for aesthetic philosophers who subscribe to the second kind of theory are often interested in the way in which art tells on the lives and minds of those who pay attention to it—but only, I think, incidentally so. Obviously most of those interested in art in any way at all are so because they think it somehow important: a philosopher of the second type may go as far as that persistent propagandist for aesthetics, Harold Osborne, who holds that "the appreciation of beautiful works of art is among the most valuable experiences of which the human mind is capable." [1] This is, one might say, an occupational claim among aestheticians, giving an air of reputability to labours that might otherwise appear barren or at least remote. But I can see no logical reason why an aesthetician as such is under any compulsion to take his philosophy into the theatre or concert hall to see what its consequences may be. If he doesn't, however, and particularly if his professional inclination is to eschew an interest in effects and to concentrate on aspects which he believes "intrinsic" to the work of art simply as an "object," one result is likely to be that his account of *why* the experience of art is so valuable will be arbitrary and unconvincing.

It is perhaps in the nature of his case that the theorist tends to bring out his examples as and when they can be used as illustrations of this or that particular point. Hence they often have the air of museum specimens, mere simulacra of the living works which people meet when they are not theorizing but reading poems or looking at pictures. These simulacra generally suit the philosopher's book well enough, at least until one begins to ask questions about the relevance of his work to criticism and practice: they are the dummies in the shopwindow, which are admirable for hanging clothes on but cannot move about and have no conversation. The critic, however, is in a very different position. Most critics have been much concerned with effects—usually the effects of particular works—and they are probably more inclined, if they want to generalize widely, to a philosophy such as, say, Mrs. Langer's than to one like Osborne's. In either case a critic rarely commits himself to a philosophy without doing a good deal of (possibly implicit) criticism first. And his deductions from this work will be the grounds for his holding to this or that general point of view.

But the critic—the "philosophical critic" I think he would sometimes be called—who goes to the length of explicitly subscribing to a definite aesthetic is in a much more difficult position than the philosopher (who is, as such, under no obligation to be a critic). The literary critic remains a literary critic, and his readers will rightly demand not only that he be consistent with his theorizing, but that he talk sense about literature.[2] The most potent danger is that he will allow his theory to dictate to his criticism, thereby reducing it to a mere application of abstract principles. In a very naïve passage a well-known critic has explained that

> The good critic cannot stop with studying poetry, he must also study poetics. If he thinks he must puritanically abstain from all indulgence in the theory, the good critic may have to be a good little critic. . . . Theory, which is expectation, always determines criticism, and never more than when it is unconscious.[3]

Of course no critic can be wholly without some general attitude toward what he studies, but it is altogether an abdication of his function for the critic to let his theory (his "expectation") settle issues for him like this. And if there is a need to be specific about theory, it is because only then will the critic know enough about his own expectations to prevent their prejudging the work in hand. At best the theoretically aligned critic is likely to be slightly schizophrenic, at worst thoroughly doctrinaire. In particular the critic who joins forces with an aesthetic which depends for its existence on a separation of the "nature" of a work of art from any relation to its public, may well find the greatest difficulty in making a real connexion between his aesthetics and valuations which need to be expressed in "human" terms if they are going to sound plausible or even relevant.

John Crowe Ransom (the well-known writer quoted above) is one of the few literary critics who have openly stated a belief in some structural aesthetic (defining works of art in terms of internal rather than relational properties) and has attempted to describe poems accordingly. It is to his credit that he has pushed the difficulties met by aestheticians on the fringes of literature to the point where their oddness becomes abundantly clear, both as a fact in itself and as something standing in the way of any real usefulness the theory might have for criticism. Ransom is an extreme objectivist whose exclusion of all human references from the "essence" of literature reaches in the end a situation in which he cannot avoid an account of value which is both subjective and personal in a sense which by this time has lost interest and stimulus. He rejects from criticism all "personal registrations,"

> which are declarations of the effect of the art-work upon the critic as reader. The first law to be prescribed to criticism, ... is that it shall be objective, shall cite the nature of the object rather than its effects upon the subject.[4]

This is the diametric opposite of such a view as that announced by Lawrence at the beginning of his essay on Galsworthy: "Literary criticism can be no more than a reasoned account of the feeling produced on the critic by the book he is criticising." It is, in fact, the opposite of any criticism which starts with the critic's own meeting with the work. But it is difficult to see what other start there could be, as before this meeting the critic has no information—no *first-hand* information anyway. Nevertheless some writers have felt that to admit as much is to surrender the essential "objectivity" of critical standards. The following note, for example, shows Osborne routing out the origins of impressionistic criticism in Pater:

> His characteristic preoccupation comes out clearly in the following passage from the Preface to *The Renaissance*: 'What is this song or picture, this engaging personality presented in life or in a book, *to me*? What effect does it really produce on me? Does it give me pleasure? and if so, what sort of degree of pleasure?' You have only to

isolate this and you have impressionistic criticism. With it may be contrasted Arnold's characterization of Clough: 'he possessed these two invaluable literary qualities—a true sense for his object of study, and a single hearted care for it. . . . In the study of art, poetry, or philosophy, he had the most undivided and disinterested love for his object in itself, the greatest aversion to mixing up with it anything accidental or personal.' Here you have in germ the two ideals of descriptive criticism—description of the subjective impressions made by the object on the critic (and so, to the extent that the critic is 'normal,' upon all competent observers) and objective. The two ideals are conveniently summed up in Arnold's phrase 'to see the object as in itself it really is' and Pater's retort that in order to see the object as it really is one must first know one's own impression as it really is.[5]

The opposition found here between the two writers seems to me largely unreal, however much difference there may be in their outlooks in general. It would be ridiculous to suggest that we can do without our "impressions"—for we only know the work of art by its effect on us. It is clearly important that we make sure that they aren't merely passing fancies, that they aren't *just* "accidental or personal"; but we have nothing else to bring us into contact with the work at all, and without this contact we have no reason to pay it any attention. Moreover Pater's question, "what is this to me?" is surely an essential one to ask if we are to produce a genuine judgment about it. We do in fact judge the importance of works of art first of all by their effect on us, on "our sincere and vital emotion" (in Lawrence's phrase), though of course the judgment, to have wide human validity, needs to be that of a sensitive and educated intelligence. What we cannot do without is the initial human *meeting* with the object: the critic has only his own and others' perceptions to go on, and "the nature of the object" for him cannot be more than the nature of the object as, firstly, he and, secondly, others see it.

Significantly enough, the statement of Ransom's quoted previously comes from an essay called "Criticism, Inc.," in which he pays tribute to the work then (in the middle thirties) being put in hand at Chicago by R. S. Crane and his team ("for the time being perhaps with a limited programme, mainly the application of Aristotle's critical views").[6] The "objective" description of the "nature of the object" may very well be undertaken as a piece of teamwork, rather like some research in a scientific laboratory. In fact it is (or was then) part of Ransom's design that critics should become "more scientific, or precise and systematic." The system here certainly seems likely to be effective in eliminating any troublesome human impulses, and it is possibly still some way from Eliot's "common pursuit of true judgment." Here is Ransom's prescription:

> Rather than occasional criticism by amateurs ["critics have nearly always been amateurs"], I should think the whole enterprise might be seriously taken in hand by professionals. Perhaps I use a distasteful figure, but I have the idea that what we need is Criticism, Inc., or Criticism, Ltd.[7]

The application of set critical (or aesthetic) views certainly fits well into such a scheme, which is calculated to oppose the inclination of the "critic as reader." The kind of criticism which Ransom specifically has in mind is "criticism of the structural properties of poetry": [8] these properties are the "aesthetic or characteristic values of literature," [9] and they turn out naturally to be independent of the substantial core of poetry, for this Ransom holds is something that it may share with prose and cannot therefore be what marks poetry out—still less what marks out each separate poem.

There is no need for a belief in objective values in art, independent of any *one* observer, to be in terms which rule out art's relation to values really existing outside itself. It is, however, oddly characteristic of "structuralist" aestheticians to have subjectivist leanings outside. Ransom's attempts to explain why we value art as we do end in fact in hedonism: there seems to be a close connexion between a kind of pigeon-hole aesthetics ("seeing each object as it really is") and an account of valuation which is helpless to generalize what appear as no better than comparatively idle personal preferences. At least one can see the forces pushing the critic from the other end: an indiscriminate valuation can of itself give rise only to an indiscriminate aesthetic—hence the need to establish an autonomy of art independent of criteria of value.

This autonomy is a matter of some urgency for Ransom. In fact the view that criticism should report on the effects of a poem upon the reader he calls "odious,"

> because it denies the autonomy of the artist as one who interests himself in the artistic object in his own right, and likewise the autonomy of the work itself as existing for its own sake . . .[10]

The critic is to ignore the reader entirely; and he is to be altogether humble in the face of the poem. His job is

> to read his poem sensitively, and make comparative judgments about its technical practice, or, as we might say, to emulate Eliot. Beyond that, it is to read and remark the poem knowingly; that is, with an esthetician's understanding of what a poem generically "is." [11]

I suggest that this degree of respect for what the poem

"generically is," for its right to exist "for its own sake," is disproportionate and, for genuine poetry, largely irrelevant. It is, moreover, very difficult to keep to, and Ransom easily slips away, as my next quotation will show. A poem in fact does not exist independently of its potential readers and its effect on them: considered in itself it is simply a thing—a collection of words, which only has significance, and meaning, in terms of the life that it celebrates, chastises, denies, or ignores. But this doubtless is the pass to which the critic who sticks to a "structuralist" aesthetic must come. In default of his being able (as many literary theorists are) quietly to forget theories when they are inconvenient, this attitude in a critic will have a disastrous effect on his technical accuracy. In fact Ransom's treatment of "technique" makes it out to be something entirely irrelevant to the main fabric of the poem:

> Studies in the technique of the art belong to criticism certainly. They cannot belong anywhere else, because the technique is not peculiar to any prose materials discoverable in the work of art. . . . technical studies of poetry . . . [would treat] its metric; its inversions, solecisms, lapses from the prose norm of language, and from close prose logic; its tropes; its fictions, or inventions, by which it secures "aesthetic distance" and removes itself from history; or any other devices, on the general understanding that any systematic usage which does not hold good for prose is a poetic device.
> A device with a purpose: the superior critic is not content with the compilation of the separate devices; they suggest to him a much more general question. The critic speculates on why poetry, through its devices, is at such pains to dissociate itself from prose at all.[12]

Technique, then, is not to be considered in relation to the poet's struggle to communicate particular experiences, because communication is incidental to the poem's "ontological" status. On the contrary, a study of technique, when carried through by a superior critic, becomes the means to discover the reason for poetry's being so full of what Ransom comes to identify as "irrelevancies." (The term fits with such a usage as "lapses" in the passage above.) This will be the critic's attempt to state some *general* aesthetic; inevitably, I think, when the discussion begins from such premises, the point of arrival will be arbitrary, if considered as an attempt to relate the significance of poetry to human values lying beyond it. Ransom would no doubt agree: for him the point is hedonism—poems are as they are because we like them that way.[13]

Ransom, then, sees poetry as disconnected from action, from any active life. Its effect is to be something of a brake, not only to distance the reader's view, but to isolate it. In *God Without Thunder* (Ransom's "primer of modern heresy," and a better book than Eliot's), he finds this to say about sensibility: "In order to be human, we have to have something which will stop action, and this something cannot possibly be reason in its narrow sense. I would call it sensibility."[14] So "aesthetic forms" are "a technique of restraint," opposed to "economic forms" (that is to say practical skills, ways of doing things). "They stand between the individual and his natural object," imposing "a check upon his action."[15] This seems to suggest some extra-aesthetic significance ("in order to be human"): yet the main function of the sensibility, of the gap in nature which it provides, is to have no function. The poem, the work of art is to be known for its own sake.

2

The attitude of (it seems to me) wrong-headed reverence for literature (and art generally)—a view which involves a serious playing-down of the value of art—is a natural outcome of the aesthetician's view of art as something whose essential qualities are *"intrinsic"* and do not derive from its relations to things outside itself. For if the "nature" or the "essence" of art removes it from the region in which we are accustomed to make valuations (a region always involving *some* human connexions), it is impossible to attribute values to it which are other than arbitrary or accidental. Ransom is not generally so innocent as to merely accept this situation. There is, in fact, a good deal that is definitely disingenuous in his elaboration of a theory apparently bluff, straightforward and uncomplicated, which turns out, nonetheless, to have much about it that is perversely sophisticated.

Aestheticians very often come to grief when they meet literature: their main difficulty is that words obviously refer to things outside themselves. Ransom, as literary critic, evidently knows that he has to pay particular attention to *meaning,* but the effort produces an account of poetry which involves complete structural dislocation, and in the end triviality. This account divides the poem into two parts: "the poem is a loose logical structure with an irrelevant local texture." [16] The description goes through a number of picturesque versions and analogies. Poems are, for example, compared with houses, whose walls are structural and whose wallpaper is decorative [17]—an analogy which shows (by Ransom's very insistence on it) how much he means us to take note of the "irrelevant." For wallpaper (decoration) can be changed without affecting the structure of the house; and this is precisely what Ransom thinks about the local texture of poetry—it too can be changed while the "loose logical structure" remains untouched. It is however the local texture which *is* the poetry. Ransom at one point refers to "those philosophically timid critics who are afraid to think that the poetic increment is local and irrelevant" and explains that

> the intent of the good critic becomes therefore to examine and define the poem with respect to its structure and its texture. If he has nothing to say about its texture he has nothing to say about it specifically as a poem, but is treating it only insofar as it is prose.[18]

To discuss the poem's structure is, then, to discuss something which it shares with prose, which in fact turns out sometimes to *be* a prose statement. The use of the word "structure" is confusing: perhaps there is some ulterior motive as if to suggest a greater coherence than Ransom's theory really allows; for it refers, of course, not to the whole poem, but to some prose statement, some subject-matter which the poem starts with (and then decorates with material irrelevant to it), whose importance is irrelevant to the importance of the poem and which can be detached and probably treated more accurately in prose. Thus in writing of Milton, Ransom remarks that his poetry

> broadly speaking may be said always to deal with "important" or highly economic subjects. But the importance of the subject is not the importance of the poetry; that depends more on the sensitiveness and completeness of the experience. The subject will generally be found to have been treated more precisely or practically somewhere in his economic prose; that is, in the ethical, theological, political tracts.[19]

"Practically" may be granted, inasmuch as in his verse Milton was not intending (as he was in his "economic" prose) primarily to move people to action. But the real interest of this passage lies in Ransom's ability to distinguish the completeness of an experience from what it is an experience *of*: the use of "precisely" is also noteworthy, as showing what a low opinion Ransom has of the ability of poetry to render experiences accurately, precisely, meaningfully.

In another image Ransom describes a poem as

a democratic state, hoping not to be completely ineffective, not to fail ingloriously in the business of a state, by reason of the constitutional scruple through which it restrains itself faithfully from a really imperious degree of organization. It wants its citizens to retain their personalities and enjoy their natural interests. But a scientific discourse is a totalitarian state. Its members are not regarded as citizens, and have not inalienable rights to activities of their own, but are only functions defined according as the state may need them to contribute to its effectiveness.[20]

It is always difficult to know how far one is intended to follow Ransom's picturesque illustrations. Here, perhaps, quite a long way, for he repeats the picture a few pages later. The truth behind it is that the very complexity of most good poems, their avoidance of easy or over-simplified effects, makes their "business" something much harder to pin down than that of a scientific discourse or a piece of economic prose (that is to say, anything that is not poetry). They are written with a less obvious or less simple purpose. For Ransom, however, the state's business and the activities of the citizens are mutually irrelevant. It is the local texture which has "personality" and this is independent of the organization of the poem, which is modest enough to let the citizens run off in whatever direction they want.

But the implications of the theory are more strikingly revealed in a passage in which Ransom is commenting on the opening manifesto of Winters' *Primitivism and Decadence*. Ransom's statement begins with another example of his refusal to admit a tech-

nique which is related in any way to the need to
communicate, to express, for the technical considerations with which he begins ("It should never be
forgotten that poetry in coming to its final form is
conditioned by technical considerations") are a matter of juggling with the meter and the "logical structure" to make them square with one another. But the
passage should be quoted in full:

A poet must do two things at once; one is to make a
logical structure, the other is to make meter. The logical
structure is ordinarily the meaning that he starts with,
having its appropriate words. But there is the meter, a
purely phonetic pattern, which requires its appropriate
words too, and cannot accept every word that comes.
The meaning-words have to be manipulated, and altered, in order to suit the meter. Eventually the poem is
done. [!] In it now the relation of the meter to the
meaning is that of a texture to a structure; this texture is
adventitious, and irrelevant to the structure, but highly
visible, and to the innocent reader like a curious increment of riches that had not been bargained for. But the
finished poem will have even more important texture
than the phonetic. It will have texture of meaning too,
and it is the requirement of attending to the meters in
the act of composing the meaning that secures this too.
Tinkering with the words loosens up the logic, introducing periphrases, ellipses, inaccuracies, and, what is much
more valuable, importations. In trying to find for the
logical detail a substitute that will suit the meter, the
poet will discover presently that the best way is to
explore this detail to see what it contains, and to come
up with facts which belong to the detail but not to the
logical structure; so a texture of meaning is established
with respect to the structure; and nothing in poetry is so
remarkable as this. It is the thing that peculiarly
qualifies a discourse as being poetic; it is its differentia.
The fact of this non-structural increment of meaning is,
I think, what critics need most to attest.[21]

Now this is a very remarkable statement. It gives a strong impression that the theory has been Ransom's first interest, and his master, while his judgments—and even his poems—are conceived as illustrations or workings out of it. This would no doubt link with the refusal to allow the critic's own response ("as reader") to come into his report of the poem. But the filling-in of the logical-structure/local-detail framework brings some most unexpected discoveries. In the first place, the nature of the logical structure is now made more explicit, and we find that it is something that already has its appropriate words before the poet does anything with it; or perhaps the sentence means that the poet first makes a statement of the logical structure in prose (a statement which would presumably be a more efficient treatment of his subject than his final poetic product). Why the poet should not be content with these appropriate words is very unclear: for some reason he wants to combine them with a "meter"—which is likewise something that comes along ready-formed, also requiring its appropriate words. I take it that this means any words that will fit the metrical pattern. For if the meter chooses its own words, and the logical structure *its* own, the attempt to fit the two together would obviously come to an immediate halt except by a spectacularly lucky chance.

Then, "the relation of the meter to the meaning is that of a texture to a structure." What can this mean? What *is* the relation of a texture to a structure? What is a texture? Ransom nowhere explains. Doubtless, as in the wallpaper illustration, he means that the chosen meter is *arbitrarily* related to the meaning, but the vagueness of the terms he uses seems designed to give, with their solemnity, an impression of special respectability. At any rate the meter is "adventitious and irrelevant" to the structure: presumably then for Ransom there could be no objection to writing an elegy in a gay triplet measure or the lightest love lyric in alexandrines. It is, however, in this "manipulation" of the meaning, this "tinkering" (fiddling about, we might say) with the words, that an entirely new "texture of meaning" crops up as well: "it is the requirement of attending to the meter in the act of composing the meaning that secures this too." These new meanings also will be haphazard and irrelevant to the structure: they will be the actions of citizens unrelated to the business of the state—"importations" as Ransom puts it. No wonder then that the logic is loosened, and that the poem will no longer treat the subject as precisely as the prose statement. At the same time Ransom remarks that the texture of meaning is "established *with reference to the structure.*" This phrase seems to me very difficult to interpret. The effect of what he has said before is to dissociate the texture of meaning from any but an accidental connexion with the structure: the two do not work in conjunction, but rather against one another, often resulting, one must suppose, in a most unproductive tension. It appears indeed to be their mutual irrelevance which "peculiarly qualifies the discourse as being poetic." Mixing meanings like this sounds easy enough to do; but it is difficult to understand why anyone should embark on it with more seriousness than he might give to devising a crossword puzzle.

What I believe Ransom means by the difficult phase is that the logical structure now acts as a loose framework within which can be hung the new and irrelevant texture of meaning. This at least is how Ransom analyzes the relation of structure and texture in some lines in *Macbeth* (I.vii. 61 ff.).

Lady Macbeth says she will make the chamberlains drunk so that they will not remember their charge, nor keep their wits about them. But it is indifferent to this argument whether memory according to the old psychology is located at the gateway to the brain, whether it is to be disintegrated into fume as of alcohol, and whether the whole receptacle of the mind is to be turned into a still. These are additions to the argument both energetic and irrelevant—though they do not quite stop or obscure the argument. *From the point of view of the philosopher* they are excursions into particularity. They give, in spite of the argument, which would seem to be perfectly self-sufficient, a sense of the real density and contingency of the world in which arguments and plans have to be pursued.[22]

But these details are very relevant, not indeed to Lady Macbeth's plan as she sees it, or to her "argument," but to the placing of these within the play. This "miniature plot process" (to use Kenneth Burke's excellent phrase) reflects some of the central issues of the play and reinforces the density of *its* meaning. For here memory as "the warder of the brain" is in the position of the guards whose failure to protect Duncan comes from their minds' having become a fume; that the seat of *reason* should have become a still is indeed directly appropriate here at the exact moment where reason and the sense of order in the protagonists themselves are being overcome by heady and uncontrolled passions. It is not *in spite of* the argument that, as Ransom says, these details give "a sense of the real density and contingency of the world in which arguments and plans have to be pursued." They in fact put the "argument" into its context (something which the "philosopher" might not like): this last sentence of Ransom's seems to me to summarize neatly just that function of "texture" that he has been denying.

In this case the outside pressure of Ransom's theory has not altogether prevented him from seeing what the poem is about. At other times I am not so sure. Writing of King's "Exequy" (a poem which he seems to like) he says that at one point the subject disappears into "the image of an impatient seventeenth-century explorer-traveller, following across land and sea a lady who has made an incomprehensible journey to an ocean paradise in the West." I take it that this must be meant ironically; for it is incredible that anyone with Ransom's literary experience should miss the point of the metaphor here, or its relation to the setting sun, the sun which has been so prominent an image of King's dead wife earlier in the poem. But such a metaphor as "my West of life" is the very opposite of a submerging of the subject: it is, on the contrary, the bringing of it into the open, the crux at which we see fused all that his wife's death means to King, personally and theologically. Perhaps there is *something* arbitrary about King's image—that is, about the whole extended metaphor in which the poem exists: another one *might* have been devised, though it is hard for us to think of any that would make us as keenly aware of the poignancy of King's feeling of loss at the same time as we register his religious resignation and acceptance of the natural order, so that he will not hasten his own death however he may desire it. It is a combination of these that this whole metaphor seems to offer us uniquely. But Ransom's theory makes it impossible to see the "structure" of a poem *in terms of* metaphor, as in such a case as this we must. He sees no use in metaphor save for decoration, and so he is led to a silly literalism which conceals the actual meaning of the words. His theory has provided him with blinkers which are peculiarly disabling in a critic of poetry.

3

Ransom seems at times to be aware that his theory makes it difficult for him to explain why it is that we should continue to take any interest in poetry. He is evidently disappointed in it (it is "only make-believe"), and over and again he asks himself the question, which he never explicitly answers: why should the poet or reader bother himself with such stuff?

> Speculative interest asserts itself principally when we ask why we want the logical substance to be compounded with the local substance, the good lean structure with a great volume of texture *that does not function*. It is the same thing as asking why we want the poem to be what it is.[23]

There seems indeed no possible answer, when the issue is put in those terms, except that for some unaccountable reason one happens to like it that way. And in fact this is the answer that Ransom gives—an answer which he admits is subjective, and which thereby rules out the possibility of linking a poem's (objective) "nature" with its value. Where the "final desideratum" for the critic is "an ontological insight, nothing else," the appeal of interest cannot be other than arbitrary or personal:

> A beautiful poem is an objective discourse which we approve, containing objective detail which we like.
>
> This version mixes objective and subjective terms, but goes much further than simply to say that poetry is a form of discourse which enlists our favorable emotions. It tells where the favorable emotions come: in the pleasure of handling the specific detail while we are attending effectively to the whole. It talks about what we like, and I see no overwhelming necessity to do that, for we shall not have poems, nor things in poems, unless we like them; liking is interest, and ultimately I suppose it is part of our unarguable biological constitution.[24]

As Winters has pointed out, liking is certainly not the same as interest; but Ransom is evidently committed to something that he cannot explain as more than a stubborn fact, individual or biological. Of course there *are* stubborn facts; but this gesture gives up the search for understanding altogether too easily. The criterion of beauty in poetry is "liking" (for the "approving" is only attached to the objective discourse, which is the same as the logical structure and so a matter of prose statement). We "take pleasure" in handling the detail, and so on. Cultivation of sensibility on this level has led Ransom into some very unfortunate remarks, perhaps in an attempt to make aesthetics look more presentable. "Sentimental and aesthetic attitudes" are, he says, "nearly indistinguishable in their final analysis." Consequently we find this:

> We consider it monstrous if one does not acquire a sentimental regard for one's brother, or mother, or close business associate; close principally in the sense that we frequently encounter the person and become acquainted with his personal quality. But one is not immoral, strictly speaking, in not having this regard; Kant would have thought that having it was a moral weakness. One is simply deficient aesthetically.[25]

I do not suppose that this is entirely fair to Kant: if it is, it is hardly to his credit. And the conclusion with its air of fastidious refinement and superiority to normal human feelings cannot be explained away (as in the following quotation from Edward Bullough) by any special sense that "aesthetic" might be thought to carry. Bullough's claims for aesthetics may seem extravagant:

> What we call tact is essentially a form of behaviour actuated by aesthetic habits of thought and feeling. What might be termed the education of the heart, as distinct from the education of the intellect, means the development of our aesthetic sensitiveness to life. Cul-

ture, as distinct from learning, education in its fullest
sense, pure humanity, with what is best and without
what is worst in human nature, rests fundamentally
upon such an education of the heart, upon such an
aesthetic philosophy of life.[26]

We may justly feel that he has extended the meaning
of the term in an unusual and perhaps confusing way;
but at least he has not devalued humanity. Ransom's
statement, on the other hand, suggests far too much
the moral dilettante for one to be satisfied either with
his aesthetics or with his idea of morality. And in fact
aesthetic considerations have throughout been treated
as essentially trivial.[27]

4

A great deal of Ransom's criticism has been
actively concerned with limiting the field of aesthetics
and making explicit its divorce from the work of the
"moralist." His defence of the poem's autonomy, his
insistence on ruling out its effect on the critic as reader,
his discussion of technique without reference to its
function as a medium of communication or expression
(denying indeed that this is its function), his analysis
of poetic quality only in terms of a texture irrelevant to
what moral substance the poem's logical core may
possess: all these can be seen as facets of Ransom's
dissociation of himself from the moralists whom he
evidently considers as his chief opponents. Moreover,
while blaming the incidence of confusion on the
"planners of society" in the past, he sees "modern
poetry" as setting itself free from bondage to morality.
The poet's traditional function on behalf of society
was, Ransom says, "to make virtue delicious."

He compounded a moral effect with an aesthetic effect.
The total effect was not a pure one, but it was rich, and
relished highly. The name of the moral effect was

goodness; the name of the aesthetic effect was beauty. Perhaps these did not have to coexist, but the planners of society saw to it that they should; they called upon the artists to reinforce morality with charm. The artists obliged.

When they had done so, the public did not think of attempting to distinguish in its experience as reader the glow which was aesthetic from the glow which was moral. Most persons probably could not have done this; many persons cannot do it today. There is yet no general recognition of the possibility that an aesthetic effect may exist by itself, independent of morality or any other useful set of ideas. But the modern poet is intensely concerned with this possibility, and he has disclaimed social responsibility in order to secure this pure aesthetic effect. He cares nothing, professionally, about morals, or God, or native land. He has performed a work of dissociation and purified his art.

. . . .

The modern poets intend to rate only as poets, and would probably think it meretricious to solicit patronage by making moral overtures.[28]

Ransom's irony, of which we have here (I believe) an extended example, always tends to be a double-edged weapon: it comes as something of a surprise to find, a moment later, that he himself disapproves of this trend among modern poets. (In an analogy elsewhere he likens poetry more to salt than lemonade, inasmuch as it is a compound, not a mixture, the properties existing separately only in our minds, after we have performed an act of "qualitative analysis.") However that may be, "moralizing" seems to be a very simple business. Ransom illustrates his distinction in the present case with comments on a "pure" poem (Stevens' *Sea Surface Full of Clouds*) and an "obscure" one (Tate's *Death of Little Boys*), to which Winters has made a very adequate rejoinder.[29] One of the oddest and most interesting of Ransom's remarks is his suggestion that Tate has deliberately roughened and obscured his poem ("roughening" is something that he also thinks happened to *Lycidas*): "Tate, as if conscious that he is close to moralizing and senten-tiousness, builds up deliberately, I imagine, an effect of obscurity." [30] This is not much excuse for the tortuous-ness of this bad poem, though it is interesting as an extreme example of the doctrine of irrelevancy. Ran-som himself prefers the obscure poetry to the pure—a preference not based on any aesthetic superiority but arising because the obscure poetry has a "more excit-ing" subject. On Ransom's own terms, therefore, this liking has nothing to do with the poems as poems. But his inability to relate the preference to anything in the nature of the poem itself—or what he would refer to as its poetic texture—is due to his extremely simplistic view of the way in which poetry involves moral or human issues. Yet he certainly describes some of his preferences in terms which suggest that he really is talking about the poem as a whole and not just its subject matter. Intellectually at least, he makes no sharp dividing lines:

> I can see no necessity for waiving the intellectual stand-ards on behalf of poets. If Dante's beliefs cannot be accepted by his reader, it is the worse for Dante with that reader, not a matter of indifference as Eliot has argued. If Shelley's argument is foolish, it makes his poetry foolish. In my mind Dante's beliefs are very bold speculations at which the accusing finger has pointed steadily for a long time now, but substantively are better grounded, and methodologically far more consistent, than Shelley's beliefs. That consideration would enter into my preference of Dante over Shelley. [31]

This is a very sensible observation. But if the foolish-ness of Shelley's poetry comes from the foolishness of his argument, then the local texture is certainly suffering because of the weakness of the logical structure. There is no longer a suggestion of mutual irrelevancy; and in this mood it is not surprising to find Ransom claiming that "the defense of poetry in the last resort, like the defense of religion, will have to be a defense of its human substance." This, we have been more recently told,[32] is the problem that faces the critic. So we should all have supposed. Perhaps this is simply a rationalization of Ransom's "preferences," perhaps a recognition that his treatment of poetry cannot altogether leave them out.

Ransom in fact continually uses words such as "importance" or "rightness," which must imply that "human substance" is to be taken into account. The essential difficulty that Ransom (so far as I can discover) has never faced is to find out how. His references to the moralist's characteristic behaviour are of a kind to make one fear the most starchy analysis. It is hardly surprising to find that "it would be quite premature to say that when a moralist is obliged to disapprove a work the literary critic must disapprove it too"[33] where the moralist is described as one (among others) "who professionally ignore individuals and concern themselves with classes and laws." This is the moralist identified with the moral philosopher, and no doubt *his* professional standard alone would be inadequate equipment for a literary critic. Ransom elsewhere refers to the poem's ethics ("if it seems to have an ideology"), as if the moral content of a piece of literature were a philosophy of morals. Of course it might be, though Ransom is doubtless right in general that "the straight ethical consideration would be prose." But this still does not mean that the moral philosopher's enquiry would be what we should mean either by moral criticism, or by literary criticism of moral issues in a poem.

When he is not thinking of philosophy, Ransom

sees the moralist's standpoint as sectarian: he is there to "apply standards," not to find the human qualities involved. And this application is consigned to the reviewer, not the critic: "The moral standard applied is the one appropriate to the reviewer; it may be the Christian ethic, or the Aristotelian one, or the new proletarian gospel." [34] Naturally enough Ransom finds that the result of an enquiry like this will be to exclude some of the content. I agree that if this is what is meant by moral criticism of literature, then it is certainly not what should be meant by literary criticism; for genuine criticism can never be the *application* of external standards of any kind. Yet if literary criticism implies too some reference to moral content, even perhaps discussion centred on moral terms and moral issues, the distinction may be hard to draw.

We get a revealing indication of just *how* hard it may be, and at the same time how necessary for the critical spirit, in Leavis' extremely interesting discussion of Eliot's *After Strange Gods*:

'The number of people in possession of any criteria for distinguishing between good and evil,' writes Mr Eliot, 'is very small.' As we watch his in use, we can only test them by reference to our own surest perceptions, our own most stable grounds of discrimination. When, for instance, he says that he is 'applying moral principles' to literature, we cannot accept those principles as *alternatives* to the criteria we know. 'What we can try to do,' he says, 'is to develop a more critical spirit, or rather to apply to authors critical standards that are almost in desuetude.' The first phrase is strictly accurate: we could recover such standards only by the development — *as* the development — of a more critical spirit out of the capacity for discrimination that we have already. To put it another way: moral or religious criticism cannot be a substitute for literary criticism; it is only by being a literary critic that Mr Eliot can apply his recovered standards to literature. It is only by demonstrating convincingly that his application of moral principles leads to a more adequate criticism that he can effect the kind of persuasion that is his aim.[35]

At first glance this might look hypercritical: there might be occasions when "applying critical standards" would be an acceptable (if loose) way of referring to the need to keep up standards in practice, to exercise a critical spirit. (Arnold spoke, fairly enough, of the "application of ideas to life.") But this is not one of those occasions: we notice that Eliot *prefers* his second phrase ("apply critical standards") to his first—that is to say, he writes as if it were a more accurate way of making his point. If he is "applying moral principles," the context seems to go out of its way to make clear that the standards exist and are fixed for the reader (the critic) prior to his experience of the work he is concerned with. Of course the most innocent and inexperienced reader does not come to his reading naked of sentiment or conviction. And if the Eliot who "applies moral principles" is too like Ransom's "reviewers," it may be hard to find a way between him and the opposite extreme represented by Ransom himself. Leavis asks elsewhere that the critic bring to bear as much "experience of life and literature together" as possible. Experience of life is, in a wide sense of the word, moral experience; and we do not generally think well of the man whose actions in no way depend on principles. In what way, then, do we bring this experience to bear in the judgment of art and in particular of literature, without committing ourselves to the "application" of standards"? The issue is momentarily crystallized in the distinction that Leavis makes when he says that we cannot accept moral principles as *alternatives* to the criteria we know; it is a point of great fineness and great importance, and I shall be largely occupied with it in the next three chapters. What follows here is the initial discussion of a few elementary issues.

At the opening of a paper called "Religion and Literature," which has already received a great deal of hostile comment, Eliot wrote:

> Literary criticism should be completed by criticism from a definite ethical and theological standpoint. In so far as in any age there is common agreement on ethical and theological matters, so far can literary criticism be substantive. In ages like our own, in which there is no such common agreement, it is the more necessary for Christian readers to scrutinize their reading, especially of works of imagination, with explicit ethical and theological standards. The "greatness" of literature cannot be determined solely by literary standards; though we must remember that whether it is literature or not can be determined only by literary standards.[36]

This essay was apparently written with a theologically inclined audience in mind, though it has been twice reprinted in general collections of Eliot's prose. In the conditions of its first appearance, the opening sentence *may* be acceptable for particular purposes. Literary criticism is not the whole of life, and there may indeed be room for other kinds of comment, where these are not offered as a substitute for firsthand literary judgment. That Eliot *does* see them as a substitute is a suspicion which is confirmed in the rest of the passage quoted and more generally in the whole essay. "In so far as in any age there is common agreement on ethical and theological matters, so far can literary criticism be substantive."

The sentiment here is elusive, but the basic point should, I think, command general assent. "Agreement on ethical matters"—if we take that phrase in a generous light—gave substance, for example, to literary criticism in the Augustan period. And if we were to rephrase Eliot's sentence, it could be made much more acceptable, without perhaps essentially changing his meaning: "only when there are commonly held moral conventions, a common acceptance of certain values—in life as in literature—will standards exist for the literary critic to appeal to." The great question for Eliot is: to what does the critic appeal when these conventions, this common acceptance, are not to be found? (I say "for Eliot": Leavis, I think, would either say that in such circumstances there is *nothing* to appeal to, or would point to particular works of literature, inviting an agreement which would itself imply accord on substantial human values.) And Eliot's answer, for himself and his fellows, is that

> In ages like our own, in which there is no such common agreement, it is the more necessary for Christian readers to scrutinize their reading, especially of works of imagination, with explicit ethical and theological standards.

In so far as this merely amplifies the first sentence, it must mean that the Christian reader has to follow something called "literary criticism" with a check on whether the literature is in harmony with Christian ethics and theology—that is, with what is, for Eliot, a system to all intents fixed both in theory and practice, and antedating, or at least logically prior to, any experience of literature. And the last sentence of his paragraph must then mean that the "greatness" of literature is determined in the light of explicit ethical and theological standards—established independently of the literature under judgment. Eliot puts "greatness" in quotation marks, but what is this a concession to? The so-called "literary standards" that we are offered at the end are no longer, under any possible reading, the standards of literary criticism. And the likely effect of his application of explicit theological standards is obvious enough from what he writes near the end of his paper:

> For literary judgement we need to be acutely aware of two things at once: of "what we like," and of "what we *ought* to like." Few people are honest enough to know either. The first means knowing what we really feel: very few know that. The second involves understanding our shortcomings; for we do not really know what we ought to like unless we also know why we ought to like it, which involves knowing why we don't yet like it. . . .
>
> It is our business, as readers of literature, to know what we like. It is our business, as Christians, *as well as* readers of literature, to know what we ought to like. It is our business as honest men not to assume that whatever we like is what we ought to like; and it is our business as honest Christians not to assume that we do like what we ought to like.[37]

The only thing, surely, that can be taken from this is that there are certain things—and certain things only—which the Christian ought to like for reasons which stem from his being a Christian, and which presumably do not hold for other people. Christianity, in short, is laying down conditions ahead of experience, setting up standards to be applied; and the reader can hardly be blamed if Eliot's mode of expression seems to propose something in the nature of an Index of Books that we (or Christians) are permitted to like.

Vincent Buckley, also writing from an explicitly Christian viewpoint, has argued that religious criticism has no need to be inflexible—or indeed theological:

> Surely Christianity is relevant as a form . . . of life guiding and enlivening our own native responses: guiding *because* it enlivens them. If that is so, then it need not involve the erection of a 'standard,' which is permanently and unalterably 'there'; and anyone observing the

process of our critical judgment from the outside would be hard put to it to see it as a specifically Christian criticism.[38]

Yet if the critic's Christianity "enlivens" his responses, "guiding" them this way rather than that, his criticism must to that extent be coloured by it, must be specifically Christian. If there is nothing by which the outside observer may distinguish the Christian critic from his peers, it is hard to see why he should be called by a special name. Buckley, of course, emphasizes the *process* here. I hope he is right in what he says on this point. But even if the process of judgment is indistinguishable among Christian and non-Christian critics, they start from different convictions, and it must be that the finishing point will also to some extent be different.[39]

This is inevitable, and it would be foolish to regret it or to try to argue away the existence of principles. Moreover every work of literature—every work, that is, of any size—takes a huge complex of things for granted: everything that the meaning of the words contains for us inasmuch as we are human, all the human qualities that a living man or woman brings with him just because he is human. When Leavis argues that the critic "is concerned with the work in front of him as something that should contain within itself the reason why it is so and not otherwise," [40] he cannot mean to exclude from this "content" all that its meaning necessarily involves for its readers. And of course it is to an aspect of this that Leavis refers in his appeal to our "profoundest ethical sensibility." We all bring much that we hold in common; and the work of art is a *particular* focussing of this. But we are all different in our backgrounds, outlooks, capacities, knowledge—and consequently in the slants that these press on us; and the urgent question that always has to be faced is: where does the invocation of what we bring with us cease to be relevant and become instead an impertinence? We can certainly say that anything *merely* private or eccentric ought to be inadmissible; but a writer's religious—or political—persuasion should be much more than that. Insofar as these persuasions are a summary, a focussing, of certain of the attitudes which have been developed through his experience, they rightly have their influence. Yet for the literary critic, the experience which counts is of "life and literature together." And the short general answer (for there will be a particular one in each meeting between a reader and a piece of literature) to the question just asked is that what we bring with us becomes an impertinence when it involves the *imposition* of sectarian or particular values. Leavis himself is not, in the passage referred to, open to the charge of imposition; for having involved our ethical sensibility, he goes on: "If of course [an author] can work a revolutionary change in that sensibility, well and good." It is this kind of flexibility which the *professionally committed* critic, whether Christian or Marxist or anything else, cannot allow himself: the flexibility which allows the work to make its own impact on a sensibility genuinely open to receive it.

It appears to me that Eliot in the essay discussed above is in this position. Yet, addressing a very different audience, he ended a later lecture:

> it is ultimately the function of art, in imposing a credible order upon ordinary reality, and thereby eliciting some perception of an order *in* reality, to bring us to a condition of serenity, stillness, and reconciliation; and then leave us, as Virgil left Dante, to proceed toward a region where that guide can avail us no farther.[41]

So here it is art—not ethics or theology—which imposes an order enabling us to see order *in* reality. What order we see thus depends much on the effect the art has on us. *This* emphasis, surely, is the one for the literary critic to make on this issue—an emphasis on a form of judgment by which the work is allowed to play on our unfettered sensibility. Yet this is not to see the sensibility, the responding mind, as a blank slate on which the work makes whatever imprint it pleases. As Leavis says in introducing his study of part of the tradition of English poetry, the account "must, to be worth anything, be from a clearly realized point of view," [42] A point of view may, of course, be doctrinal. Leavis, on the contrary, insists on the primacy of "that of someone living in the present": a sensibility alive to its own time (though not necessarily limited to its conventions and the commonplaces of its modes of thought). As an example of the sensitivity possible under this definition, I cite Leavis' essay on *Measure for Measure*.[43] The play represents for him a "challenge . . . to our deepest sense of responsibility and our most comprehensive and delicate powers of discrimination." [44] Throughout the essay he asks (in effect), "What challenge does this make to us now? What judgment does such and such an action compel in the circumstances presented in the drama *as Shakespeare presents it?*" The complexity of response required by the play (with its corollary of a great suppleness and tact in making the necessary literary judgments) is a challenge to be met not with dogma or from rigid principle, but with "our most comprehensive and delicate *powers* of discrimination." And it is this flexibility which allows the critic to register accurately the subtle balance of judgment which Shakespeare himself makes. Thus, of the attitude to law proposed by the play as a whole, Leavis writes,

to believe that some organs and procedures of social discipline are essential to the maintenance of society needn't be incompatible with recognizing profound and salutary wisdom in 'Judge not, that ye be not judged,' or with believing that it is our duty to keep ourselves alive to the human and personal actualities that underlie the 'impersonality' of justice. Complexity of attitude isn't necessarily conflict or contradiction; . . .[45]

I think that this essay is a fine example of a sensitive critic allowing a work of art to have freedom to work its influence on his own mature judgment, refining, sensitizing, making possible ever more delicate discrimination. Yet to lay proper stress, even in many examples, on the importance of this (however necessary it may be initially) is far from settling by itself the problem of relevance opened by the question asked a few pages back: when does it cease to be relevant to invoke what we bring with us to the meeting with a work of art and become instead an impertinence?

Leavis has observed in his essay on 'Johnson and Augustanism' that the ability to be relevant in literary criticism

implies an understanding of the resources of language, the nature of conventions and the possibilities of organization such as can come only from much intensive literary experience accompanied by the habit of analysis.[46]

This, I think, is not to be disputed. Yet by itself it is hardly sufficient. For we have to consider the ends to which the resources of language are put. Thus Winters, calling himself a "moralistic" critic, announces his view of purpose in literature while (unintentionally) giving the clue to a major limitation in his work. As he puts it,

a poem (or other work of artistic literature) is a statement in words about a human experience. I use the term *statement* in a very inclusive sense, for lack of something

better. But it seems to me obvious that *The Iliad,
Macbeth* and *To the Virgins to Make Much of Time* all
deal with human experiences. In each work there is a
content which is rationally apprehensible, and each
work endeavors to communicate the emotion which is
appropriate to the rational apprehension of the subject.
The work is thus a judgment, rational and emotional, of
the experience—that is a complete moral judgment in so
far as the work is successful.[47]

I shall argue later that this attitude involves Winters in
a disastrously shortsighted view of the "resources of
language." Yet at the same time his emphasis on the
significance of the moral judgment in literature seems
to me certainly correct. Leavis' own work is full of
open or implicit acknowledgment of this fact. And it
seems to me that—to take one example at random—he
is obviously right that "there must be something important to say about the moral seriousness of George
Eliot's novels; otherwise she would hardly be the great
novelist one knows her to be"; to ask for the "moral
substance" "definable in terms of human interest," to
call George Eliot "simply a great artist—a great novelist, with a great novelist's psychological insight and
fineness of human valuation."[48] These are the only
terms in which intelligent discussion of literature can
be carried on, and to accept *their* relevance is a necessary condition of being able to account seriously for
art's being credited with any essential human importance. An aesthetic theory which separates art from life
and denies the relevance of moral comment on the
aesthetic performance "relegates art," as Winters puts
it, "to the position of an esoteric indulgence, possibly
though not certainly harmless, but hardly of sufficient
importance to merit a high position among other
human activities."[49]

But the problem of moral relevance cannot be

settled quite out of hand. Commenting on the closing sentence of Professor Sutherland's introduction to the Twickenham *Dunciad*—"the criticism of the nineteenth and twentieth centuries has been far too much concerned with the moral issues raised by Pope's satire, and too little interested in its purely aesthetic values."—Leavis observed that

> 'Aesthetic' is a term the literary critic would do well to deny himself. Opposed to 'moral,' as it is in this sentence, it certainly doesn't generate light. Moral values enter inevitably into the appreciation of the *Dunciad*, if it is judged to be a considerable work; the problem is to bring them in with due relevance, and the bringing of them in is the appreciation of Pope's art.[50]

The "due relevance," particularly in such a case as Pope's, calls for the greatest sensitivity, for "our own surest perceptions, our own most stable grounds of discrimination" are indeed all that we have. I have suggested the dangers of losing sight of these in making judgments on literature from a position of externally wrought strength; and it is, incidentally, a danger that may lead to the worse one of allowing literature to become the tool of social or political orthodoxies. The *use* of literature, whether by Zhdanov or more mildly by Raymond Williams, is a natural derivative of surrendering it to the care of moral or political dogma. The writer's moral responsibility becomes instead a matter of political or religious orthodoxy; and in losing its integrity literature gives up both its rights and its function as "nutrition of impulse," as incitement to humanity "to go on living" (in Pound's phrase). For, as Winters has written in a fine passage, poetry

> should offer a means of enriching one's awareness of human experience and of so rendering greater the possibility of intelligence in the course of future action; and it

should offer likewise a means of inducing certain more or less constant habits of feeling, which should render greater the possibility of one's acting, in a future situation, in accordance with the findings of one's improved intelligence. It should, in other words, increase the intelligence and strengthen the moral temper; . . .[51]

There is a (doubtless accidental) emphasis here which might be regretted. The last sentence is indeed very impressive. But to see literature as "a means of inducing certain more or less constant habits of feeling" may invite a *use* of poetry as pernicious as any other. I do not believe that Winters had this in mind, but his statement does imply that we know where we are going, or what it really means to "strengthen the moral temper." It implies that we not only know what it is to have, as Arnold puts it, "a central, a truly human point of view," but that we are in touch with it and in an important way share in it. Perhaps we do. Yet to bring it to bear on our criticism, on our judgment of literature, remains something calling for the greatest tact and for a sense of relevance, the nature of which is as hard to set down as ever it was.

2   STRATEGIC SELECTION:
CRITICISM BY CHOICE OF TERMS

IT IS NATURAL to find the keenest interest in making *use* of literature among those committed to particular political (or, less often, religious) programmes. This can be clearly recognized for instance in the work of Christopher Caudwell and—at least in his earlier manner—in that of Kenneth Burke. If I choose to discuss the problem in the context of an avowedly Marxist critic's writing, this is not through special prejudice, but rather because the outlines of Marxist criticism are usually particularly sharply drawn and can be easily identified and (to use a favourite word of Burke's) charted. At the same time there are, as far as I know, very few literary critics who are explicitly liberal or conservative in their professional writing. This is no doubt in the nature of the case, for the Marxist prescription is so much more rigid and (in one sense) so much more comprehensive than its rivals' that it is only here that the total political impression can be received. Moreover, Burke's attitude to the aims of criticism has led him to devise a methodology (not restricted in its use to a Marxist approach) whose technique relates very closely to his own exterior purpose: thus the effect of keeping the purpose constantly in view can be studied through examining the tactics of the method.

The central concept on Burke's critical theory is that

of the literary *act* or literary action. So, in one of his prefaces, he remarks that

> The quickest way to sloganize this theory is to say that it is got by treating the terms "dramatic" and "dialectical" as synonymous. So it is, as you prefer, to be called either "dialectical criticism" or "dramatic criticism methodized" (i.e., a reasoned method for treating art as act).[1]

There are obviously many kinds of act which literature can be thought of as embodying. Here, for example, is a representative passage from Caudwell:

> the developing complex of society, in its struggle with the environment, secretes poetry as it secretes the technique of the harvest, as part of its non-biological and specifically human adaption to existence. . . . Without the ceremony phantastically portraying the granaries bursting with grain, the pleasures and delights of harvest, men would not face the hard labour necessary to bring it into being. Sweetened with a harvest song, the work goes well. Just because poetry is what it is, it exhibits a reality beyond the reality it brings to birth and nominally portrays, a reality which though secondary is yet higher and more complex. For poetry describes and expresses not so much the grain in its concreteness, the harvest in its factual essence . . . but the emotional, social and collective complex which is that tribe's relation to the harvest. It expresses a whole new world of truth—its emotion, its comradeship, its sweat, its long-drawn-out wait and happy consummation—which has been brought into being by the fact that man's relation to the harvest is not instinctive and blind but economic and conscious. Not poetry's abstract statement—its content of facts, but its dynamic rôle in society—its content of collective emotion, is therefore poetry's *truth*.[2]

This is an account of origins (the history is perhaps suspect), but, by a process common in Marxist writing, Caudwell extends it to cover the present nature of poetry. The account, crude as it is and vitiated by the genetic fallacy,[3] does nevertheless have one great advantage. As Marius Bewley has written in another context,

> Literature is, in such a view, brought into an arena of the widest significance, and theoretically its participation in life is complete—or rather, literature *is* life in an entirely realistic way. Poetry is therefore seen to be ethical, and of the deepest influence in shaping 'our structures of orientation.'[4]

Of course this is nothing new: the virtue of any approach which involves it will lie partly in any freshness that a restatement from a different point of view can bring to an idea discredited, often, simply because it is worn, but mainly in the lead it can give in meeting literature itself. Yet too definite an orientation will always tend to represent literature as something other than itself; and the main danger of "sociological" criticism will be a tendency to use and distort literature for political ends. For Burke, meaning itself is bound up essentially with programmes of action and seems in fact to be defined in terms of them. The reading of a given meaning will then depend for its sensitivity on the comprehensiveness of the programme to which the critic is dedicated. And the accuracy of his judgment will, on this view, be a measure of its relevance to the programme implied by whatever attitude is involved in the presentment of the meaning.

It is not really surprising that only in their more generalized statements are critics who look on literature with a particular social or political programme in view altogether acceptable. In this respect Burke is very much more adequate than Caudwell. He is a shrewder man and obviously has a wider and more intensive literary experience. He rarely allows himself the particular openings which Caudwell is often so glad to walk into: in fact his political self-commitment is much less explicit at all times. He has, also, enough subtlety in his understanding of the powers of litera-ture (of what ways it will allow itself to be used) to see that crude categorizing defeats its own end. And he can, in his curious way, speak out for what he calls poetic (as opposed to semantic) meaning, and for the virtue of letting art impose its own order of life:

> If a dismal political season is in store for us, shall we not greatly need a campaign base for personal integrity, a kind of beneath-which-not? And I wonder whether we might find this beneath-which-not in a more strenuous cult of style. This effort has been made many times in the past—and as regularly has been despised at other times, when there was no longer any need for it. Style for its own sake? Decidedly, not at all. Style solely as the *beneath-which-not*, as the *admonitory and hortatory act*, as the *example* that would prod continually for its completion in all aspects of life, and so, in Eliot's phrase, "keep something alive," tiding us over a lean season. And there is all the more reason for us to attempt doing what we can by *present* imagery, since the promissory, the rewards of "postponed consumption," hold out so little of encouragement for the political future within our lifetime. So might we, rather than living wholly by a future that threatens so strongly to refute us, do rather what we can to live in a present that may in good time spread into the future? [5]

"A strenuous cult of style" is not a phrase which will please many people. What I understand Burke to be after here is an increased attention to the power of words, by their selection, to determine an attitude in the writer, affecting thus at least part of his meaning. For Burke goes on to attack the kind of blank styleless writing (of editorials or business letters) which he now sees has become the norm, the writing of the trained opinionator, of whose opinions he asks:

> have they done anything? Can they, in this form, possibly do anything? I submit that they cannot. And further, I submit that, in so far as they become "the norm," they serve to prevent the doing of anything. On the other hand, out of attempts to key up the values of style, there could emerge writers whose muscularity was a fit with the requirements of the people. As things now stand, "the norm" prevents even an attempt at such selectivity.[6]

Burke's rhetorical questions are possibly a conscious reminiscence of one of Arnold's favourite critical approaches. Elsewhere, Burke has shown some sense of superiority to Arnold as well as an imperfect acquaintance with him.[7] But the essay from which these extracts come (it is called 'Semantic and Poetic Meaning' and shows Burke at his best) appears to be, like much of Arnold's work, an attempt to bring the training of the literary critic to bear on more general social problems. If the measure of Burke's limited achievement as a critic, interesting though it is, is in some respect that of the decayed ambience of his generation, it is more clearly (in comparison with Arnold) a mark of his inferiority in sensitivity, suppleness, and general intelligence. Arnold would hardly have allowed himself to talk in terms of a "strenuous cult of style," of "writers whose muscularity was a fit with the requirements of the people." But then Arnold has a less simple view of these requirements and is less easily able than Burke to tolerate the encroachments of "the norm." Taking up the rhetorical questions, one may ask: what, granted the situation as you show it, have *you* done? What, with your kind of approach, can you do? And if the answer is disproportionately slight in comparison with the intellection and the effort em-

ployed, it will not do simply to answer that the en-
thronement of the norm of the "semantic ideal" has
ruled out the possibility of anything better. Burke's
intellectual muscles are indeed formidable. Yet he
hardly has the critical tact to use them in such a way as
really to benefit society. He does not bring the literary
critic's sensitivity to his treatment of social and political questions. Even in so interesting an essay as that on
Hitler's *Mein Kampf,*[8] what we have is essentially a
politician's approach—serious, sensible and straightforward, but very much taking the human issues for
granted. Possibly in such a case, extreme as it is, they
might be so taken; yet this is always a dangerous thing
to assume, and Burke here has the opportunity to do so
much more: just how much one can judge, for instance, from Lionel Trilling's excellent essay on the
Kinsey report[9] in which the critic's skill is used to
bring into prominence just those delicate human
aspects which Kinsey, through his (quite deliberate)
selection of method, had chosen to consider irrelevant
to his case.

Burke, it may be said, though he sometimes knows
the right questions to ask, has not sufficient faith in
literature to let it give its own answers. His understanding of the *general* situation in which poetry finds
itself today is, I think, sound enough. But in almost
every statement of this theme come expressions which
reveal the strong arm of the politician who has already
made up his mind. Thus he deplores the effect of what
he calls the "semantic ideal" in writing:

> Above all, it fosters, sometimes explicitly, sometimes by
> implication, the notion that one may comprehensively
> discuss human and social events in a nonmoral vocabu-
> lary, and that perception itself is a nonmoral act. It is
> the moral impulse that motivates perception, giving it
> both intensity and direction, suggesting *what to look for*

and *what to look out for.* Only by wanting very profoundly to make improvement, can we get a glimpse into the devious personal and impersonal factors that operate to balk improvement. Or, stating this in reverse, we could say that the structural firmness in a character like Iago is in itself an evidence of Shakespeare's moral depth.[10]

The main burden of the first two sentences here is a point of great importance, which is very little understood. It is presented precisely and clearly; and if the antitheses ("what to look for/what to look out for") seems a little too glib, it has its usefulness in pointing to the genesis of the insight of a Shakespeare: only, we may ask, does it say more than that Shakespeare's awareness of the possibilities of good gave him an equal understanding of the realities of evil? I think that, critically speaking, it ought not to. Burke's purpose in choosing his phrases seems to derive from his consciously restricted aim, an aim whose character emerges to some extent in his desire to "make improvement": this is the kind of approach which those who have experienced Burke's writing in any quantity will immediately suspect of bringing in—however casually—the illicit categories of previous political persuasion.

On several occasions Burke explicitly identifies the literary critic with the political activist. Here is a passage which almost by itself reveals most of the implications which his "programme" will have for the survival of literature:

Our own program, as literary critic, is to integrate technical criticism with social criticism (propaganda and didactic) by taking the allegiance to the symbol of authority as our subject. We take this as our starting point, and "radiate" from it. Since the symbols of authority are radically linked with the property relationships, this point of departure automatically involves us in socio-economic criticism. Since works of art, as "equipment for living," are formed with authoritative structures as their basis of reference, we also move automatically into the field of technical criticism (the "tactics" of writers). And since the whole purpose of a "revolutionary" critic is to contribute to a change in allegiance to the symbols of authority, we maintain our role as "propagandist" by keeping this subject forever uppermost in our concerns. The approach, incidentally, gives one an "organic" view of literature, sparing him the discomforts of discussing the "social" and the "technical" as though they were on two different levels. He spontaneously avoids a dualism of "form" and "content," "beauty" and "use," the "practical" vs. the "esthetic," etc. He gets a unitary approach to the matter of dialectal interaction.[11]

Here any conception of criticism as the handmaid of literature is entirely wanting: from being a free play over all the issues that literature may raise, criticism has become "revolutionary," the servant of a particular faith, committed to and directed by it. This commitment appears in the present case to be established at the start by the "subject" chosen. (The book is *Attitudes Toward History*, but Burke nevertheless writes explicitly as a *literary* critic.) The subject, that is to say, is a natural for the Marxist-orientated writer whose political concerns are uppermost. Since all real or substantial questions are socio-economic, only by seeing the "technique" of literature in the light of them can we link technical and social criticism.[12] The latter, we note, is identified with propaganda and didactic; and here we have the explanation of Burke's limitations in such essays as that on *Mein Kampf*, as well as a key to his particular success there—he is able to meet Hitler, at least partially, on his own ground. But the force of the argument in this passage, with its repetitions of "since" and "automatically," is seen to be spurious when we understand that "socio-economic criticism" is going to issue not only from taking as one's subject allegiance to the symbol of authority, but from allegiance, per se, to one firmly defined political persuasion. It is quite clear, then that as criticism is subjugated to a political programme, so art must be sacrificed to propaganda. There is no escape from the unitary approach; to call it organic looks like a calculated take-over of the word on a level with the streamlining of the argument.

Indeed Burke is quite explicit on the primacy of the social or political determinant. We learn that sociological classification

> would consider works of art, . . . as strategies for selecting enemies and allies, for socializing losses, for warding off evil eye, for purification, propitiation, and desanctification, consolation and vengeance, admonition and exhortation, implicit commands or instructions of one sort or another. Art forms like "tragedy" or "comedy" or "satire" would be treated as *equipments for living* that size up situations in various ways and in keeping with correspondingly various attitudes.[13]

According to such a definition, art will be judged good if it can be used profitably in any of these ways. But what is perhaps most striking here is the phrase "equipments for living" (which Burke himself italicizes). It is not a pretty phrase, but its mechanical appearance is not accidental. Burke's language in fact continually betrays him into the hands of his ostensible enemies, the purveyors and the technicians of the norm. In arguing against the twentieth-century victory of technology, he writes that "technological efficiency has become too like psychological inefficiency"; and one notices the frequency with which such words as "automatic" come into his vocabulary. When human life is considered in terms of "psychological efficiency" it is not surprising that art has become a technique of organization to certain very definite, previously determined, ends.

For Burke "living" needs to be rather minutely defined and accounted for, before it becomes an acceptable reference; living is not just living—it is living in certain precisely marked out ways. Hence the pressing of literature into the service of a pre-determined cause.

> If we are to revise the productive and distributive patterns of our economy to suit our soundest desires, rather than attempting to revise our desires until they suit the productive and distributive patterns, it would surely be in the region of poetry that the "concentration point" of human desires should be found. The corrective of scientific rationalization would seem necessarily to be a *rationale of art*—not however, a performer's art, not a specialist's art for some to produce and many to observe, but an art in its widest aspects, *an art of living*.[14]

One does not need to start with any particular dislike of the objects of Burke's propaganda to feel that an art of living defined in the language in which he habitually writes is going to have very little breadth or resilience. That a literary critic should have a convinced and well-defined attitude to life is not in itself cause for complaint, though one may legitimately ask that it should not be a rigidly limiting one: he must take sides on some issues, see things as right or wrong, as desirable or undesirable. What I have in mind to object to in Burke is that his social and political beliefs, far from being in some way drawn out of his critical findings, and moulded by his experience of literature, have fixed the direction in which the criticism is to develop and stunted the natural growth that it might have had. Critical thought follows in the wake of political and is dedicated to supporting an established doctrine. Thus one comes to notice certain unsatisfactory emphases in remarks which may otherwise appear harmless. "There are," Burke observes,

> two general bases of critical exhortation. (1) We may have a concept of an ideal situation, and insist that literature be written in accordance with this ideal situation; or (2) we may have a concept of a contemporary situation, and insist that literature be written in accordance with this contemporary situation. The first method is absolutist: it seeks to determine once for all what kind of literature is categorically superior to what other kinds of literature. The second method is relativistic, or historical: it holds that if literature is to be written for an ideal situation at a time when the actual situation is far from ideal, writers must sacrifice the appositeness of art in the interests of a purely academic conception of "perfection." [15]

To an ear already warned by "equipment for living," such a phrase as "the appositeness of art" may well sound like a plea for art as propaganda in favour of a situation not contemporary but to be developed partly through the medium of art, directed to this set purpose. And if one is inclined at first to ask what it is to write literature "in accordance with" a "situation," the answer is likely to be that it is to write deliberately to affect the situation in certain specific ways. I believe that when the *Counter-Statement* essays were written, Burke had not developed his "strategy-situation" terminology, but there is no need to look for a substantial change. Literature written in accordance with a situation (ideal or contemporary) will be regarded as consisting of strategies for "selecting allies," "socializing losses," and so forth—inescapably with the intention of producing specific change *in accordance with* an already formulated doctrine or set of beliefs: it is in this that we shall find the appositeness of art to con sist. The "situation," that is to say, includes the judgment of itself in terms of a particular orthodoxy. More indeed, it includes not only the judgment but also the motives for action *and therefore the action itself*. "Situation," Burke claims, "is but another word for motive." Now there is a sense in which this is obviously true, but there is some equivocation in the passage from situation in its original sense to motive and action. "Situation" seems originally to have meant to Burke (the "ideal" or the "contemporary" situation) the state of things as they are or as they might ideally be. A complete map of the situation would presumably include all actual motives whether or not they had been realized in action. But this is evidently not what Burke intended in his reference to literature written "in accordance with" a situation. The slight shift in meaning has thus enabled him to give a deterministic account of motives, so making the writer a tool of the contemporary situation. Situation determines motive; motive determines action.

Hence, though he does not say as much explicitly, it is impossible to avoid the impression that if the "two general bases of critical exhortation"—the "ideal" and the "contemporary"—are to be distinguished and opposed Burke will have a clear preference for the second. But there is no good reason why they must be opposed. This would only be the case if the "accord" meant that the writer is to be bound by some orthodoxy to a specified kind of report on the contemporary situation, whereas the accord that matters is that the writer's work should be his own sincere response to life as he experiences it. Such an experience, or perception, must be (as Burke has rightly insisted) itself a moral act—which is to say, in the terms of the present discussion, that it will imply reference beyond itself to some conception of an "ideal": not a fixed academic idea of perfection, but the writer's own sense of relative values which has developed through his own gathering of experience. His perception on each occasion is an act which involves naturally his past experience and thus becomes placed among others of its kind, affecting and being affected by them.

Such a statement would hardly be activist enough to satisfy Burke, though he does on one occasion say that "the artist—as artist—is not generally concerned with specific political issues." Nonetheless, as he goes on, what the artist *is* concerned with implies economic and political choices:

> He may sing of pastoral moments on the shores of the Mississippi, nothing more; but if the things he extols there are found to be endangered by the growth of chain stores, his purely pastoral concerns involve by implication the backing of an anti-chain store candidate for President. Thus a system of aesthetic subsumes a system of politics.[16]

This illustration is disarming enough, called out, surely, to enlist all our inbred pieties. What to some extent it conceals is that Burke elsewhere takes it for granted that the judgment on the "system of politics" is necessarily a comprehensive judgment of the "system of aesthetics"—that to disapprove of chain stores is all one with appreciating Mark Twain. There are times when Burke apparently sees men as limited within the bounds of a political agent; and then we may adapt (to rather different ends) a remark of Ransom's already quoted and observe that there is no automatic reason for the literary critic to approve or disapprove whatever the political theorist does. Burke's choice here of a homely and simple illustration is obviously calculated. At the same time it is much *too* simple to do more than act as a very generalized slogan; for it is not the character of literature to raise political issues in such elementary ways, but rather to explore and light up the complex human situations in which the inevitably simplifying political decisions have to made. The critic's post (as such) ought to be with the involved human situation rather than the narrow political act—asking questions which are more fundamental than any particular politics of the day.

Before looking further into Burke's methodology, it is worth referring briefly to an idea which occurs in his first book, *Counter-Statement,* before the situation-strategy formula was worked out, though not before he was seeing literature as politically directed. In talking of a "Lexicon" that he was (not very seriously) considering, he writes that it

> would not for the world make literature and life synonymous since, by comparison in such terms, the meanest life is so overwhelmingly superior to the noblest poem that illiteracy becomes almost a moral obligation. Rather, our "Lexicon" would look upon literature as the thing added—the little white houses in a valley that was once a wilderness.

In the preface to the second edition (written twenty-one years later) Burke takes himself to task for the passage I have just quoted:

> in keeping with my later cryptological interests, on looking over the original Preface I'd incline to ponder now the closing reference to literature as "the thing added . . . wilderness." I'd incline to ask: "How does this writer use 'white,' 'houses,' 'valley,' and 'wilderness,' in other contexts?" And I'd wonder whether he had had remotely in mind the line in the Sonnets: "By adding one thing to my purpose nothing." [17]

One might retort that the interests of anyone spending time on Burke are bound to a certain extent to be cryptological also. It might seem impertinent to question him further on this context, since he himself seems to doubt what the earlier passage means: but the later criticism is even more obscure. And one important question is to my mind left out. I'd incline to ask: "How does this writer use 'added' (together with all the other words) not in other contexts but in this one?" The difficult line from a difficult sonnet does not help, since it is not clear whether the quotation is a wry comment on the inadequacy of the former statement, or whether Burke thinks that the word "added" is being used in the same sense by Shakespeare and by himself. Does the quotation (as here used) mean that the addition of literature is nothing to the purpose, or is it just that the preface adds nothing to the book? That it adds little more than a puzzle is true enough. Certainly we want to know what "white" and the rest are doing, for we want to know how, through the addition of the houses, the wilderness became something very different, if it is Burke's contention that the meanest life is in some way made less mean by literature.

This idea of literature as an addition crops up later in the same book, and it seems to conflict quite sharply with the active function with which he elsewhere credits art:

> once one is taught to seek in art such experiences as one gets in life itself, it is a forgone conclusion that one must discover how trivial are artistic experiences as compared with "real living." A mere headache is more "authentic" than a great tragedy; the most dismal love affair is more worth experiencing in actual life than the noblest one in a poem. When the appeal of art as method is eliminated and the appeal of art as experience is stressed, art seems futile indeed. Experience is less the *aim* of art than the *subject* of art; art is not *experience*, but *something added* to experience. But by making art and experience synony-

mous, a critic provides an unanswerable reason why a man of spirit should renounce art forever.[18]

Just how much is being said here? For "experience" we must read, presumably, "direct experience of the thing the art is relating or showing" (since clearly one experiences art in a perfectly ordinary sense): but then the distinction between a "real" loveaffair and one in a poem is obvious to the point of dullness (though it does not follow that it is always more worthwhile to have a dismal loveaffair than to read of one in a poem—it all depends). Of course art is not the same as life; and indeed to say that a headache is *more authentic* than a great tragedy only confuses the issue. For a tragedy is not "authentic" at all in the way that a headache is; it is not happening in real life, and to compare the two (commenting on the triviality of the art-experience) is in fact to make a simple mistake in classification—a "type-error," as it would be called in logic. What can, obviously, be compared are the experiences of having a headache or keeping a date with the experiences of watching a tragedy or reading a poem. And then, though one cannot live on poetry and must sometimes have headaches and loveaffairs, it will not necessarily follow that one would not on occasion rather read a poem than have a headache or go to a tragedy even though it means breaking a date.

But the point is obvious enough. How then does the tragedy sometimes become more worth going to? How is art "added to" experience? Not, for Burke, by merely being another experience: it is an experience to be undergone with a definite end in view.

2

Burke describes his general approach to literature as "pragmatic" in the sense that

It assumes that a poem's structure is to be described most accurately by thinking always of the poem's function. It assumes that the poem is designed to "do something" for the poet and his readers, and that we can make the most relevant observations about its design by considering the poem as the embodiment of this act.[19]

If we take the idea of "doing something" loosely and widely enough, this might be fairly innocent, a way (if a rather unusual one) of stressing the importance of *effects*. But Burke's emphasis on "function" and later on "purpose" makes it clear that he sees each work as having some particular and specific goal (not necessarily always consciously understood by the poet). The critic's methodology, which works along a parallel course, will, then, be designed to display this very busy conception of function; and the exposition will be along lines clearly marked out by the critic's "perspective" which "implicitly selects a set of questions that the critic considers to be key questions." [20] And

Implicit in a perspective there are two kinds of questions: (1) what to look for, and why; (2) how, when, and where to look for it. The first could be called ontological questions; the second, methodological. A critic eager to define his position should attempt to make his answers to these questions as explicit as possible, even at the risk of appearing to "lay down the law." After all, there are "laws" (or at least, rules of thumb) implicit in the critic's perspective—and the critic should do what he can to specify them as a way of defining that perspective.[21]

Rules of thumb are not laws (which, I think, belong more among a critic's "ontology" than his methodology). We have seen something of Burke's laws, something of what he looks out for: it is closely bound up with a set of previously settled socio-political beliefs. The rules, which derive from the notion of the poem with its clear function turn out to be more than a methodological shorthand: by their very use they implicitly decide important critical or precritical questions.

A suitable point of departure is the opening of the long essay called "The Philosophy of Literary Form."

> Let us suppose that you ask me: "What did the man say?" And that I answer: "He said 'Yes.'" You still do not know what the man said. You would not know unless you knew more about the situation, and about the remarks that preceded his answer.
>
> Critical and imaginative works are answers to questions posed by the situation in which they arose. They are not merely answers, they are *strategic* answers, *stylized* answers. For there is a difference in style or strategy, if one says "yes" in tonalities that imply "thank God" or in tonalities that imply "alas!" So I should propose an initial working distinction between "strategies" and "situations," whereby we think of poetry (I here use the term to include any work of critical or imaginative cast) as the adopting of various strategies for the encompassing of situations. These strategies size up the situations, name their structure and outstanding ingredients, and name them in a way that contains an attitude towards them.
>
> This point of view does not, by any means, vow us to personal or historical subjectivism. The situations are real; the strategies for handling them have public content; and in so far as situations overlap from individual to individual, or from one historical period to another, the strategies possess universal relevance.
>
> Situations do overlap, if only because men now have the same neural and muscular structure as men who have left their records from past ages. We and they are in much the same biological situation. Furthermore, even the concrete details of social texture have a great measure of overlap. And the nature of the human mind itself, with the function of abstraction rooted in the

nature of language, also provides us with "levels of generalization" (to employ Korzybski's term) by which situations greatly different in their particularities may be felt to belong in the same class (to have common substance or essence).[22]

Richard Blackmur has remarked that Burke's method "could be applied with equal fruitfulness to Shakespeare, Dashiell Hammett, or Marie Corelli." Burke thinks that Blackmur is right.[23] I am not altogether sure what "fruitfulness" means in this context. I think that perhaps the method is more suited to Dashiell Hammett whose incorporated situations and strategies are so much simpler than Shakespeare's and follow a more easily recognizable pattern. But, surely, Burke's method has equal validity outside literature: it could be applied to any deliberate action whatever. This of course is nothing against Burke: he would regard it as a point in his favour—and, I think, rightly so:

> The method . . . automatically breaks down the barriers erected about literature as a specialized pursuit. . . . Sociological classification, as herein suggested, would derive its relevance from the fact that it should apply both to works of art and to social situations outside of art.[24]

At the beginning of this chapter I remarked that a whole-hearted reorientation like Burke's has, for all its defects of detail, the virtue of restating vigorously the critical fact that poetry is not "pure" (in Ransom's sense), but an experience at one with all human action. As Burke here points out, the breaking down of the barriers follows "automatically" from the assumption of the method. Method (which can here be equated with terminology) is in Burke very closely linked with the more fundamental claims that his general theory of literature makes. But the effect of

Burke's choice of vocabulary is in itself to cut the lifeline of any aesthetics which depend on a separation of art from life. Now critical action by choice of terms is clearly very sophisticated behaviour: it seems to me likely to occur, on the one hand, where the writer can count on a large measure of implicit agreement in his audience on the assumptions involved in the activity of criticism—at the height, that is, of an assured civilization, where the terminology is a normal expression of universally accepted standards. (For example it will probably appear, in a disguised form as a commonplace among Augustan reviewers.) But on the other hand—and this may be one reason for Burke's adoption of the method—it can be a desperate measure for shocking people into attention, precisely when there is no agreement on standards at all.

As a tactical weapon such a device may have much usefulness. But on a longer view the terms must be selected with extraordinary care if they are not to lead to quite gross distortions. Burke's terms hardly answer this test.[25] He is of course right that "situations"—even quite complex ones—do substantially overlap, though I doubt whether they ought to be described in the brisk generalizations that he favours. His method, he observes,

suggests a variant of Spengler's notion of the "contemporaneous." By "contemporaneity" he meant corresponding stages of different cultures. For instance, if modern New York is much like decadent Rome, then we are "contemporaneous" with decadent Rome, or with some corresponding decadent city among the Mayas, etc. It is in this sense that situations are "timeless," "non-historical," "contemporaneous." A given human relationship may be at one time named in terms of foxes and lions, if there are foxes and lions about; or it may now be named in terms of salesmanship, advertising, the tactics of politicians, etc. But beneath the change in particulars, we may often discern the naming of the one situation.[26]

But this picking out of the "situation" in common between New York and Rome can in general only be done by violating or suppressing the human detail which makes the situation a human one. (Burke sounds at times much like Ransom's idea of a moralist—interested only in laws and classes.) For we need to know *how far*, and *in what respects*, New York is like decadent Rome. We cannot simply ignore the difference in setting; for a difference between foxes and lions, on the one hand, and salesmen and politicians, on the other, may be quite enough to make two different situations in any sense in which the term is critically worth keeping. Burke's repeated description of his method as "codifying" situations is suspicious. It suggests artificial simplifications, and we suspect that humanity is being bullied into conformity, its idiosyncracies and characteristics sheared off to make a neater pattern. That we have the same neural and muscular structure as men of past ages will not prevent the "levels of generalization" from being also levels of elimination of what is characteristically human about the *human* situation. And I doubt how far the *biological* situation can legitimately be invoked. Is it really still the same?

Now Burke recognizes that situations can be classified in all sorts of ways: which one you choose depends on the end in view. Consequently the reason for making such and such a classification already incorporates the kind of action which it is to give rise to. So the strategy encompasses the situation as Burke says; and since the "situation" means the situation as perceived by the strategist, situation and action inescapably involve one another.[27] Now there seem to me two things which it is important to understand about

the word "strategy" as used by Burke. The first, no-
ticed already, is that it implies some definite end to be
attained (though not, I think, one that need be stat-
able outside the work that incorporates it). Secondly,
it has unavoidable associations which suggest enemies
to be outwitted as well as forces to be deployed. Burke
takes this in his stride, but the result most certainly is
that the formula hardly survives the asking of the first
serious question about what it means. As soon as one
tries to relate it to any individual work, the military
associations show up as simply a nuisance, and one
realizes the formula's uselessness to do more than
generalize about attitudes.

By way of defending his choice of terms, Burke
quotes three definitions of "strategy" (characteristically from two dictionaries and a French treatise on
chess), embodying his definitions thus:

> surely, the most highly alembicated and sophisticated
> work of art, arising in complex civilizations, could be
> considered as designed to organize and command the
> army of one's thoughts and images, and to so organize
> them that one "imposes upon the enemy the time and
> place and conditions for fighting preferred by oneself."
> One seeks to "direct the larger movements and opera-
> tions" in one's campaign of living. One "maneuvers,"
> and the maneuvering is an "art." [28]

I think the proper corrective to this is short and simple.
Perhaps the work of art *could* be so considered; but in
the doing, it will lose all the qualities which make it a
work of art. For art is not a battle, and to look on it as
an organized campaign in the war which is life involves
one in the crudest of devaluations. The limited range
of genuine opportunities for criticism by fists quickly
brings Burke's dealings with literature to grief:

> sociological criticism . . . might occasionally lead us to
> outrage good taste, as we sometimes found exemplified

in some great sermon or tragedy or abstruse work of philosophy the same strategy as we found exemplified in a dirty joke. At this point, we'd put the sermon and the dirty joke together, thus "grouping by situation" and showing the range of possible particularizations. . . . I'll go a step further and maintain: You can't properly put Marie Corelli and Shakespeare apart until you have first put them together. First genus, then differentia. The strategy in common is the genus. The *range* or *scale* or *spectrum* of particularizations is the differentia.[29]

I think the outrage to good taste is less serious than that to good sense. Recalling the definitions of "strategy" invoked a little earlier in the same essay, we find that we are invited to agree that Shakespeare and Marie Corelli prefer the same time and place and conditions for fighting, that they organize and command the armies of their thoughts in the same way, that they share a way of directing the larger movements and operations in their campaigns of living, and that both manoeuvre. Who, in such company, is the enemy? What side are Shakespeare and Marie Corelli fighting on? Is it necessarily the same side? It is not sufficient simply to say that Shakespeare has immeasurably greater range or scale or "spectrum": the division appears such that it just is not true that they must first be put together. Comparisons and groupings are only worth making when they shed light on one topic or the other. There is not much point in measuring an ant against a lion: and the scale that includes both will tell little of interest about either. (They are of course both animals; and Shakespeare and Marie Corelli were both writers.) Moreover one might say that certain differentiae differ so widely as to begin to constitute different genera.

As an indicator of general attitudes (provided one can first get rid of irrelevancies of association) this terminology may have a limited use. At least, as we saw, it has made clear Burke's stand on the nonautonomy of literature. But its usefulness stops there: for close individual judgment it is a failure. As soon as we get down to details we are faced with the problem of "sizing up situations, naming their structures and containing in our naming an attitude towards them." Possibly one might dub a poem or a novel the naming of an attitude. But it must be clear that "naming" will not do as more than a preliminary gesture which must be extended, elaborated, and clarified in quite different terms. Only where the situations are very simple or the strategies attempted very simpleminded should we find this language suitable. Thus the novel-as-an escape-from-the-miseries-of-life might be briefly categorized: situation, a world of woe; attitude, let us forget it for a few minutes if we can; strategy, story about life in high society or long ago or on an idyllic island. Of a more complex case, Burke has this to say:

> A work like *Madame Bovary* (or its homely American translation, *Babbitt*) is the strategic naming of a situation. It singles out a pattern of experience that is sufficiently representative of our social structure, that recurs sufficiently often *mutatis mutandis*, for people to "need a word for it" and to adopt an attitude towards it. Each work of art is the addition of a word to an informal dictionary. . . . As for *Madame Bovary*, the French critic Jules de Gaultier proposed to add it to our *formal* dictionary by coining the word "Bovarysme" and writing a whole book to say what he meant by it.[30]

A dictionary is where we go to look up the meaning of a word, that is, how to use it. It would be reasonable enough to hope to find the meaning of "Bovarysme" (if we came across it) by reading Flaubert's novel. But in what sense do people need a *word* for the kind of experience which the novel offers? The virtue of a novel surely lies at least as much in the particularization of one group of experiences as in its similarity to others or its representative quality. We do indeed react by (implicitly) saying, for instance, "Yes, that is how things are," or "But surely this is *not* what really counts in such a situation." A name is something by which we can quickly and easily refer to a person or a thing—a kind of shorthand to avoid circumlocutions, which can always be cashed by its definition (by dictionary or by pointing). A novel, on the contrary, is the *displaying* of a "situation," much more than the naming of it, for it aims to show us what the situation, the particular one, is like. Moreover to call it a "strategic" naming implies that the novelist would like us to understand that his attitude is: "Here is the situation as I see it, and here (by implication at least) is what I should like done about it." This, I suggest, is too gross an oversimplification to be worth much for criticism, and the linking of *Madame Bovary* with *Babbitt* perhaps shows how far its usefulness extends.

Burke's interesting attempts at analysis of the internal workings of particular plays present a rather different case. Their procedure is to be an illustration of the viewpoint summed up in a remark by E. E. Stoll, "that Shakespeare 'observes not so much the probabilities of the action, or the psychology of the character, as the psychology of the audience.' "[31] Burke therefore puts a speech into the mouth of a character, making him address the audience in the theatre directly, explaining the function, internally to the play, of various characters and actions. The "form" of the play, the way certain themes are given emphasis, how particular phrases carry their special meanings—this is seen as a deliberate working on the psychology of the audience, raising expectations which are later fulfilled, disappointed or subtly changed. I think that in one of these

"speeches" ("Antony in Behalf of the Play") Burke
has shown that this approach is really useful as a way of
demonstrating the workings of an "expanded metaphor".[32] Its chief weakness is that it takes no notice of
the poetry; and it is also true that the particular
rhetorical method seems to have no special virtue for
criticism beyond a certain entertainment value. Its
special interest for this discussion is as an illustration
of a strategy at work, for here there is a given audience
to be worked upon. This could perhaps be called
manoeuvring; the strategy of the drama, though a very
complex one, can in some degree be demonstrated. Yet
it remains a strategy *within* the play. The larger intentions of the play as a whole it does not consider: the
conclusion I would suggest is that, though Burke's
formularized method can reveal something of internal
structure when a larger intention is more or less taken
for granted, it is altogether too crude to give a satisfactory account of a poem looked at as a whole.

More silent witness to the inherent limitations of
Burke's system comes in his discussion of proverbs, in
which "naming" finds a much more satisfactory home.
Proverbs do indeed fit the situation-strategy formula
quite adequately:

> Proverbs are *strategies* for dealing with *situations*. In so
> far as situations are typical and recurrent in a given
> social structure, people develop names for them and
> strategies for handling them.[33]

It is the character of proverbs to "chart" certain type-
situations in such a way that a "strategy" for coping
with the situation is indicated. These situations are
always either highly generalized or very simple (as in
the many relating to the weather). Also the attitudes
and strategies which they propose are likewise generalized, and they almost at least hint at some *action*.

So Burke's terminology can handle them effectively.

Now Burke does admit that literature is much more complex than any proverb. Yet he asks for the analysis which has proved satisfactory at showing the work of proverbs to be extended over all literature. And he asks, "Could the most complex and sophisticated works of art legitimately be considered somewhat as 'proverbs writ large'?" [34] It is interesting that later on in the same essay (which is explicitly concerned with sociological criticism), he remarks on the relevance of his method to fables. Now fables, whether they are simple like Aesop's or relatively complex like *The Man Who Loved Islands*, are of course very close to proverbs, which sometimes serve as their morals. But fables deliberately play down the human details of the situation they confront to allow a more generalized—a more stylized—picture to emerge. To speak of poetry as "proverbs writ large" is very well if all one wants is to make a gesture about the moral function of literature. But it remains a gesture, and the answer to Burke's question, "Why not extend such analysis of proverbs to encompass the whole field of literature?" is that it would quickly reduce the whole field of literature to the status, at best, of fables. Burke wants, he says, categories that suggest the active nature of proverbs. Literature is (in a rather different sense) naturally active too, but the very complexities which have to be insisted upon each time the analogy is drawn—the wealth of material it uses, and the range of responses which it calls upon in the reader—are exactly those points which will spoil the accuracy of the comparison.

But the fact of the matter is that Burke has chosen a formula whose artificial simplicity is determined in accordance with the use he wants to make of literature. When he says that he is "simply proposing, in the social sphere, a method of classification with reference to *strategies*," [35] one recognizes immediately a bias in favour of public action, and one suspects that the classification—of human acts and human beings, as well as of literature—will be fixed ahead by the demands of *particular* strategies. ("The whole purpose of a 'revolutionary' critic is to contribute to a change in allegiance to the symbols of authority.") The strategies, when not themselves part of a political programme, are judged in accordance with it. Burke defends his method against reviewers who find intuitive leaps in his work on the ground that his classifications are "neither more or less 'intuitive' than *any* grouping or classification of social events." But it is the habit of classifying itself that in Burke is objectionable, with its tendency to dragoon people and events along predetermined lines and its fixing ahead of the conditions of art. I wrote above that Burke's choice of method was itself critical activity at an advanced stage. This activity is in reality the redirection of art in the services of propaganda, and it makes no essential difference if the propaganda is a subtle and intricate one.

YVOR WINTERS is clearly a critic of a different stamp from Burke. Yet they have something in common. Each has a marked and consistent moral commitment, though Winters' is not imported into his criticism from an external social or political position. Each has developed and made explicit a methodology of criticism, though, again, Winters does not isolate and abstract his in the manner of Burke. Something rigid, even pedantic, in Winters' approach to poetry gives him a passing similarity to Ransom, particularly in his efforts to excavate a poem's "paraphrasable content" (which seems a little like Ransom's "logical structure"), though the two men's approaches and attitudes are entirely opposed. As against both Burke and Ransom, Winters' understanding of the moral working of a poem is more consistent, more penetrating, and more human. And while there are many occasions when the weight of theory seems to have been too much for a poem to bear, it should be stressed that his various general defences of his critical position are really a philosopher's abstracts of conclusions *drawn from his own positive judgments*.

On this point Winters is explicit, insisting that only by criticism of individual poems and other works in more or less detail can we lay the groundwork for general theories.[1] And the stress which he lays on the direction taken by his thought—*from* individual experience *to* general theory—is very important for the defence of his conception of the function of criticism. Winters' "absolutism" is not a matter of prejudice, or of a doctrine dogmatically asserted, but a deduction, as he says, from his own experience. So it is not to be refuted by merely calling it names, as some of his critics have done.[2] The only answer for an opponent to make is to claim that his experience doesn't tally.

Winters, however, is prepared for this: he claims that our experiences do tally.

> Is it possible to say that Poem A (one of Donne's *Holy Sonnets*, or one of the poems of Jonson or Shakespeare) is better than Poem B (Collins's *Ode to Evening*) or vice versa?
>
> If not, is it possible to say that either of these is better than Poem C (*The Cremation of Sam Magee*, or something comparable)?
>
> If the answer is no in both cases, then any poem is as good as any other. If this is true, then all poetry is worthless; but this obviously is not true, *for it is contrary to all our experience*. If the answer is yes in both cases, then there follows the question of whether the answer implies merely that one poem is better than another for the speaker, or whether it means that one poem is intrinsically better than another. If the former, then we are impressionists, which is to say relativists; and are either mystics of the type of Emerson, or hedonists of the type of Stevens and Ransom. If the latter, then we assume that constant principles govern the poetic experience, and that the poem (as likewise the judge) must be judged in relationship to those principles.[3]

This statement looks as if it has the virtues of clarity and simplicity—an appearance to some extent deceptive, for some philosophical terms which Winters treats as equivalent are not necessarily so. I believe that his use of the phrase "intrinsically better" is equivocal and doesn't quite justify him in posing the dilemma as he does. For when Winters writes of *intrinsic* value he is not using the word as, say, Osborne would: on the contrary he is referring to some quality of a poem considered in relation to human nature and human experience. For Winters—as for most people—value is a relational property, linking a particular experience with a given human mind. This is not to say that the relationship is not itself objective, for it does really exist, and there is nothing in its relational nature to prevent its being susceptible to indefinite degrees of generalization. One can, that is, go on to say of a particular relation that it holds between such-and-such a poem and *all* human beings, or *all humans of a certain class*. In each case a value, described in any of these terms, could remain objective. But it would not be "absolute," as the word has, I think, generally been used. And it would only be "intrinsic" to the poem in a rather stretched sense. Winters, however, uses "objective" and "absolute" as if they were synonyms:

> The theory of literature which I defend is absolutist. I believe that the work of literature, in so far as it is valuable, approximates a real apprehension and communication of a particular kind of objective truth.[4]

I take this to mean that the truth is an "eternal truth" of high generality, one referring to an unalterable fact of human nature or of the relation of this nature to abstract qualities of goodness and order. For Winters has defined the absolutist thus:

> The absolutist believes in the existence of absolute truths and values. . . . and that it is the duty of every man and of every society to endeavor as far as may be to approximate them. The relativist, on the other hand,

believes that there are no absolute truths, that the
judgment of every man is right for himself.[5]

As this passage demonstrates, "absolute" is a word
which is likely to confuse rather than the reverse, and it
is better avoided. Used in connexion with "truth" it
can mean, I think, either of two quite distinct things.
In one sense it may be said that all truths are absolute
if we believe that all propositions are either true or
false: this would be an assertion of a particular view of
the nature of truth (one which is, incidentally, assumed universally except by certain philosophers at
professional moments): it is the so-called "correspond-
ence theory." The word "objective" would more
accurately designate this view; but an objective view of
the nature of truth can be—and normally is—held by
those who at the same time are ethical subjectivists (or
"relativists"). The objectivity consists in a relation
between propositions and facts, objective in that it is
out there in the world and doesn't depend on the
situation of the particular observer. An objective view
of value could be described in a similar way, as I have
indicated, and the two would quite naturally (though
not necessarily) go together. I find more "absolute"
accounts of value barely comprehensible; I do not
myself understand value except as a concept linking
certain objects or experiences with sentient beings.
And I don't think Winters does either. Value for him
means essentially moral value; and this is meaningless
without a human reference—a reference, that is, to
actual or possible human experience: a moral truth
must be a statement of a relation between men and
their experiences. There is no reason to suppose that
Winters would dispute this, for it is implied by all the
particular judgments he makes about literature.

But it seems to me possible that by "absolute

truths" Winters means something much more exalted
—namely, truths of universal generality. These would,
I assume, be essentially moral truths held to be valid
for all men (such as those pointed to in the Ten
Commandments), together, perhaps, with very fundamental truths about the relation of men to the nonhu-
man world or to God. Now there is a particularly
interesting difficulty in laying claim to absolute truth
in this sense. It is not just that, as Winters admits, no
human being can ever be certain of having hold of one;
rather, as we examine the possibility of objective moral
relationships, we find that the desired generality of
human reference depends very greatly on narrowly
limiting the defining situation. Thus, for example, a
man feeling himself under a particular obligation in a
given situation implicitly assumes that his moral
prompting could be generalized to the extent of saying
that any man in *an exactly similar* situation would be
under the same obligation. (If, on the contrary, he
were to say, "I feel that I am under such-and-such an
obligation, but I see no reason why another man
placed as I am should feel as I do," we should suspect
that he himself had no good grounds for feeling the
obligation.) Probably no situation ever exactly recurs;
but there are more or less close approximations, and
the closer these are, the more certain do we feel that
the moral relations involved can be translated from
one to another. On the other hand those moral axioms
which seem to claim generality of application not only
to all men but to a wide range of possible actions and
situations, turn out to be really plausible only when
they are concealed tautologies (for example, "stealing
is wrong"). The rest seem to admit of so many excep-
tions, conditions, and limitations that we are forced to
believe that, in moral issues, circumstances always alter
cases.

Now if it is true that moral relationships can only be
defined with any precision when situations and conditions are made particular, this has an important bearing on literature. It accounts for our finding the greatest human value in those poems which bring a given
situation vividly before us. In the next chapter I discuss
Leavis' near-identification of "reality" and "sincerity,"
which bears closely on this issue. The point I want to
make here is in a sense a more elementary one. We feel
the moral pressures of a situation most keenly when we
can see ourselves into it, when we know it in full
particularity. So those poems which limit and define
such a situation quite narrowly are—paradoxical as it
may seem—those in which experiences coming from
the widest range of human attitudes can meet. If we
think of a poem like Hardy's *After a Journey* or a play
like *Macbeth,* we realize that it is through their very
particularity that the moral situations can be appreciated for what they are, and that the reader's own
moral sense is thereby brought most delicately into
play and sensitized. It is the particular triumph of the
poet to realize the moral situation so exactly and
delicately that the reader can recognize it as, in a sense,
his own, but his own perceived and defined with a
sensitivity of judgment which under normal circumstances he cannot command. In comparison, the poem
of more general moral exhortation or statement
usually seems more remote as the reader's own moral
imagination is less engaged.

I believe that there is a close connexion between
Winters' special interest in "absolute truths" of very
wide generality and his tendency to prefer poems
presenting general moral issues to those focussed on a
particular. Had he looked more closely at the *kind* of
moral presentation which can bring different human
experiences close together, he might better have un-

derstood the stress laid by other critics on the need for the poet's experience to be in some sense present within the poem itself, present, that is, as the object of a particular act of moral perception. I think it is only in this light that the argument of the following passage will have much force:

> if values cannot be measured, they can be judged; and the bare existence of both art and criticism shows the persistence of the conviction that accuracy of judgment is at least ideally possible, and that the best critics, despite the inevitable margin of difference, and despite their inevitable duller moments, approximate accuracy fairly closely: by that, I mean that great men tend to agree with each other, and the fact is worth taking seriously. I am more or less aware of the extent of the catalogue of disagreements that might be drawn up in reply to such a statement, but it is far less astounding than, let us say, the unanimity of the best minds on the subject of Homer and Vergil, particularly if we accept the doctrine of relevativism with any great seriousness.[6]

There will perhaps be a tendency for an opponent to retort that the best minds may be agreeing here by definition—by their agreement we recognize them as the best minds. Furthermore, there is a slightly unpleasant sense of hardening in such a paragraph, suggesting as it does that judgments gradually become fixed through time, made sure for posterity. "Accuracy," as Leavis observed, "is a question of relevance"; and if the great minds approximate it closely, what they share is a recognition of the wide range of human experience which really can, and does, meet in such works. In responding to the *Iliad* and the *Aeneid*, they are accepting them, that is to say, as human documents in which men and their experiences come together, not as storehouses of absolute truth. Only thus can they have value for us in the particular situation in which we find ourselves.

Now the central position which he gives to value is, I think, one of the most significant aspects of Winters' criticism: "the primary function of criticism is evaluation." [7] Since Winters takes it for granted that evaluation will be in moral terms, he is committed to what he calls a moralistic concept of literature, which he finds "has been loosely implicit in the inexact theorizing which has led to the most durable judgments in the history of criticism." [8] This view of literature Winters distinguishes sharply from three others, including the "didactic"; and it is not clear to me that the distinction should be drawn at this point: the didactic view is surely just a limited version of the "moralistic." Curiously enough, much of Winters' own criticism has a definitely didactic tone: I believe this to be a result of his insistence on *theory*; and his fondness for a systematic sorting out of rational from emotional content has not always allowed the poem's complete moral statement to get through. He states emphatically that "unless criticism succeeds in providing a usable system of evaluation it is worth very little," [9] and there is a real danger of the "usable system" turning treacherous if theory gets an upper hand. [10]

2

The actual critical process which Winters has in mind is extremely strange:

It will consist (1) of the statement of such historical or biographical knowledge as may be necessary in order to understand the mind and method of the writer; (2) of such analysis of his literary theories as we may need to understand and evaluate what he is doing; (3) of a rational critique of the paraphrasable content (roughly, the motive) of the poem; (4) of a rational critique of the feeling motivated—that is, of the details of style, as seen in language and technique; and (5) of the final act of judgment, a unique act, the general nature of which can be indicated, but which cannot be communicated precisely, since it consists in receiving from the poet his own final and unique judgment of his matter and in judging that judgment. It should be noted that the purpose of the first four processes is to limit as narrowly as possible the region in which the final unique act is to occur.[11]

To judge by the last sentence, and by the paragraph which follows it, these five processes are distinct, and they are presumably in chronological order: at least the final unique act of judgment can only occur when its region has been limited by the first four processes. One aim of Winters' scheme seems to be to restrict the effect of the initial act of perception (which is not included): inevitably this act will involve *some* judgment, which is likely to be modified by the later process. But it will also *affect* the process, suggesting certain broad issues to look out for, and making preliminary preferences. By eliminating this initial meeting with the poem, Winters evidently hopes to reduce the effect of unguided judgment; but he makes a plan that is psychologically inconceivable.

Perhaps even more serious are the results of his explicit separation of processes (3) and (4). If, as Winters (rightly, I think) believes, "the creation of a form is nothing more nor less than the act of evaluating and shaping (that is, controlling) a given experience," [12] the experience cannot be approached by the critic except through the form the poet has given it. Technique (or style) cannot be rationally criticized except in the terms of the experience, nor the experience seen except by way of the technique. The poet's perception of his subject-matter (which here seems to be roughly equivalent to Winters' paraphrasable content or "motive") is essentially his judgment on it. And the critic's judgment (process (5)) is in reality no more than the combination of (3) and (4): it is absurd to suggest that there is a further act after the critique has been made—unless it is seen as the allotting of a mark or a place in a hierarchy. And as his comparison of poems by Herrick and Marvell shows, Winters' ability to discover a "content" independent of the "feeling motivated" can lead to a gross misreading of the poet's judgment of his matter.

Winters' stress on paraphrasable content is largely responsible here. He remarks of a poem by Ralegh that it

> rests on a formulable logic, however simple; that is, the theme can be paraphrased in general terms. Such a paraphrase, of course, is not the equivalent of a poem: a poem is more than its paraphrasable content. But . . . many poems cannot be paraphrased *and are therefore defective.*[13]

Many poems, that is, have no formulable logic. But formulable in what terms? It seems to me merely doctrinaire to assert that the "logic" should be realizable (formulable) outside the poem: I agree that the "logic" must exist in the poem for it to be more than random, but I see no reason why it should be formulable in other terms than the poet has given it. In fact, since the content isn't separable from the poet's perception of it, there is really no way of stating the logic in other language without doing it violence. I'm afraid that this may sound to Winters like a typically romantic defence of obscurity; but I am not asking for logic to be abandoned, only that it should be seen in the poem and not out of it.

I have not come across any case where Winters explicitly gives a paraphrase of a poem. What it would be like we can gather from the remark that Herrick's poem mentioned above is "on the same subject" as Marvell's, with the implication that the logic is roughly the same in both, though Marvell's has more "irrelevancies." What the poems share is no more than an agreed starting place; and I think that the same can be said of most attempts at extracting a paraphrase. A poem which Winters greatly admires is Jonson's *False World, Goodnight*, a paraphrase of which might reasonably run: "I am finished with the world, which cannot hope to ensnare me again. I know all its cunning ways, how deceitful it is in everything. So how could I stay, or (having escaped) return again? No bird escaped from a cage willingly returns, so why should I, who have reason as well as nature to advise me? Nor are threats any use. I have suffered enough to fear nothing more that the world can bring. Yet I know that my case is in no way special, and I hope for no miracle. I shall bear the worst, scorning all false relief, and moreover I shall do it not by running away but by keeping my virtue firm." This is possibly a longer paraphrase than Winters might give, and, flat as I have tried to make it, it still contains just the faintest echo of the poem's proud tone and is thus perhaps more than a logical paraphrase. Yet Winters is obviously right that it is in no sense the equivalent of Jonson's fine poem. And while it does something to display the argument of the poem, this argument, though dignified and upright, is (as it appears here) quite commonplace; and I cannot see that such a paraphrase can seriously help any but the most inexperienced reader to make a satisfactory approach to the poem. What matters is Jonson's perception of the argument and the attitude of his protagonist, and these do not have any valid existence except in the poem which enshrines the perception.

3

In his accounts of the nature of poetry Winters is consistent with his view of the nature of the critical process, so that one can see that this latter is a more or less reasonable method of dealing with the kind of thing he thinks a poem is.

> A poem differs from all statements of a purely philo-sophical or theoretical nature, in that it has by intention a controlled content of feeling.
>
> . . . .
>
> A poem, then, is a statement in words in which special pains are taken with the expression of feeling. This description is merely intended to distinguish the poem from other kinds of writing; it is not offered as a complete description.[14]

The "content," as we have seen, must be able to be grasped rationally—it is the formulable logic on which the poem rests. But it does not come alone:

> The poem is good in so far as it makes a defensible rational statement about a given human experi-ence . . . and at the same time communicates the emotion which ought to be motivated by that rational understanding of that experience.[15]
>
> The work is . . . a judgment, rational and emotional, of the experience—that is a complete moral judgment in so far as the work is successful.[16]

"Statement," Winters observes, is to be read in "a very inclusive sense." Even so, the dichotomies which occur in each of these announcements are marked and dis-turbing. So far as the judgment is, for Winters, both rational and emotional, I think these two elements tend to be very much divided, if not opposed. Though he reminds us that "exact motivation of feeling by concept is not inherent in any rational statement," [17] the rationally apprehensible content of the poem stands apart to be judged on its own. Winters nowhere concedes that the emotional judgment might in any way affect our reading of the content: I think that this means that all moral judgment must be rational also. The result seems to me a theory of poetry which is not so much unbalanced as split down the middle. One need not go so far as to see Winters picturing the poet having an experience, making a rational statement and then finding the appropriate feelings; but even if the actual process of composition doesn't work like that, the implication is that in the finished poem the two are at least separable if not separate. (They can, it will be remembered, be studied separately, as a part of the critical process.)

Now an insistence on rationality is often very necessary; and Winters is to my mind ingenious and accurate in diagnosing an essential weakness of both *Finnegans Wake* and the *Cantos*, which he writes are "poems of revery . . . revery proceeds by the random association of daydream, and possesses a minimum of rational coherence." [18] In the absence of logic,

> Mr. Pound proceeds from image to image wholly through the coherence of feeling: his sole principle of unity is mood, carefully established and varied. That is, each statement he makes is reasonable in itself, but the progression from statement to statement is not reasonable: it is the progression either of random conversation or of revery. . . .
>
> . . . .
>
> I do not mean that the poetry cannot refer to a great many types of actions and persons, but that it can find in them little variety of value—it refers to them all in the same way, that is, casually. Mr. Pound resembles a village loafer who sees much and understands little.[19]

It was in reply to remarks similar to these that Pound suggested that Winters "has never heard of the ideographic method, and thinks logic is limited to a few 'forms of logic' which better minds were already finding inadequate to the mental needs of the XIIIth century." [20] Winters' reply is that

civilization rests on the recognition that language possesses both connotative and denotative powers; that the
abandonment of one in a poem impoverishes the poem
to that extent; and that the abandonment of the denotative, or rational, in particular, and in a pure state, results
in one's losing the only means available for checking up
on the qualitative or "ideographic" sequences to see if
they really are coherent in more than vague feeling. Mr.
Pound, in other words, has no way of knowing whether
he can think or not.[21]

The terms "denotative" and "connotative" crop up
frequently: as W. K. Wimsatt has pointed out, the use
that Winters and others make of them doesn't coin-
cide with their meaning in logic. Here they mean
"rational or explicit meaning" and "implicit or suggested meaning" (including association and allusion).
The interesting thing about the use of both words is
the evidence it gives of the philosophical ambition of
Winters' rationalism. The "defensible rational statement" looks likely to be a thesis defensible in a medie-
val disputation, and perhaps Pound has some ground
for criticizing Winters' view of logic. I myself should
say that the defect in this sense of the *Cantos* is that
their logic (if that is what it can be called) is a purely
private affair, which can't be checked by anyone outside Pound's mind. I think there is a difference here
between the *Cantos* and *The Waste Land*, which
Winters believes to be another exercise in the decadent manner of Pound. I should not like to be forced
to make a "paraphrase" of *The Waste Land* (which in
many ways I find a distressing poem); but I should say
that there is an implicit rationality behind its progres-
sion, which can be recognized and—in part at
least—understood without our needing to refer to
Eliot's purely private and personal associations.

There is another formula which Winters sometimes
uses to indicate the dual aspect of poetry: "The rela-

tionship, in the poem, between rational statement and feeling, is . . . that of motive to emotion." [22] The use of the word "motive" recalls Burke's identifying of situation and motive. Burke goes further than Winters and suggests, implicitly at least, that motive determines strategy.[23] Strategies are not feelings, but Burke at one point also identifies strategies with *attitudes*—a word which Winters largely avoids, though its meaning is clearly close to his use of "feeling." Now statements and beliefs can motivate a great variety of feelings: Winters talks of "exact motivation" not being inherent in a rational statement. But is "exact" a word which can be used to describe motives? Feelings are either motivated or not, and each "statement" may give rise to a number of different "feelings." In an interesting passage in *The New Criticism* Ransom writes as if emotion and object stay in a one-to-one relation:

> I have seen too many instances where literary critics . . . find the cognitive object of the poem intellectually obscure, yet claim to discover in the poem an emotion which is brilliantly distinct. I should think there is generally, and ideally, no emotion at all until an object has furnished the occasion for one, and that the critic is faking his discovery of the emotion when he can not make out its object; and that if he should try to describe to us the emotion he would find himself describing it as whatever kind of emotion would be appropriate towards a certain object, and therefore presently, before he realized it, beginning to describe the very object which he had meant to avoid.[24]

But at the end he has come very close to Winters' notion of the *appropriateness* of feeling to object. Ransom, after all, can hardly mean that there aren't plenty of emotional situations where the feeling generated seems out of all proportion to the occasion for it.

And to say that there is an appropriate emotion implies, I take it, a relation of (moral?) fitness between it
and its object. This is Winters' position. He holds that
"Any rational statement will govern the general possibilities of feeling derivable from it but the task of the
poet is to adjust feeling to motive precisely." [25] The
precision is a moral precision, for Winters also writes
of the feeling which "ought properly" to be motivated.
I think that "attitude" would be a better word to use:
it is not so loose as "feeling," which can in any case
perfectly well be used where moral issues are not
involved at all.[26] The poet's job is then to convey, with
his presentment of the occasion for his feeling, a
healthy moral attitude to it. I don't know whether
there could be said to be only one attitude ideally
healthy, but presumably if it is complex enough there
could: Shakespeare's attitude in *Measure for Measure*,
for example. This is perhaps as near as we can expect to
get to a "precise adjustment" of feeling to motivating
situation.

I think that, in different terms perhaps, any "moralistic" view of the nature of literature will come down
to something of this sort. But by seeming at least to
perpetuate a sharp division between motive and feeling, Winters tends, I think, to underrate the difficulties and more importantly the *capacities* of poetry and
further blinds himself to the merits of poetic uses of
language which are too complex to fit easily into the
statement/feeling plan or too creative to allow themselves to be paraphrased. Winters ends his first book by
observing "what I desire of a poem is a clear understanding of motive, and a just evaluation of feeling; the
justice of the evaluation persisting even into the sound
of the least important syllable." [27] It is not clear
whether the second half of this sentence means more
than that there should be no redundancies and noth-

ing should vitiate the main intention of the poem. Later Winters, writing of *Macbeth*, offers a slightly different formulation:

> That which makes it a living simulacrum and a living judgment is the emotion resulting from this rational grasp of the theme. Ideally this emotion should be appropriate to the action at any given stage, and the final emotion should be appropriate to our realization of the significance of the whole.[28]

Winters' critical limitations are at their most marked when he is writing of drama, as I shall indicate later. For the moment I suggest that an "adequate grasp of the theme" of anything so profound and complex as *Macbeth* will be more than just rational, and that in such a case "statement" or "theme" is not discussible in isolation from the feeling it gives rise to. I believe in fact that this is true of any poetry whose use of language is genuinely creative, though it is not always as clear as in *Macbeth*. Even in those passages in the play which are what Leavis calls pieces of "ordinary mature Shakespeare," our understanding of the theme needs to be more than discursive, and when we come to a speech such as "If it were done when 'tis done," an attempt to make a paraphrase would only produce a grotesque parody of the meaning: the action on us of such a passage as "pity like a naked new-born babe" cannot possibly be analyzed into separate cognitive and affective aspects. Taken at their face value (and their face is very often shown to us), Winters' analysis and process will distort any but the simplest poetry; and I am inclined to think that the idea of a "final emotion . . . appropriate to our realization of the significance of the whole" is one of those gestures whose air of impressiveness depends on our not asking too insistently what they mean.

Winters holds that the lyric or short poem is superior to all other forms because of its very high generality. This is an aspect of his theory that I have already
discussed to some extent, though what he actually says
at the start of *Primitivism and Decadence* doesn't
commit him to the kind of generality that he elsewhere
seems to defend.[29] But he also makes it a point of the
superiority of the lyric that it is "the expository concentration of a motivating concept, in language such that
the motivating concept and motivated feeling are expressed simultaneously and in brief space." [30] What is
involved in this notion of simultaneity is by no means
obvious: I think that it means that the description of
the concept is in terms which convey the feeling, for
no description can be neutral, and the poet takes care
that his gives an accurate account of his moral perception of his theme: his moral perception *is* his grasp.
Winters' insistence on the rational seems to have
prevented him from taking this essential point. He
seems to me very largely to ignore the *tone* of a poem,
which may vitally affect our understanding not only of
the poet's attitude to his theme, but consequently of
the theme itself (in so far as the two can be separated).
To insist on the importance of tone is to imply that the
theme, the poet's attitude to his subject, and his
attitude to his readers are not things which make sense
in isolation. This does not imply that, in assessing the
poem, one must take the poet's word for what he feels.
On the contrary, it is frequently defects in tone which
give the spurious poet away more clearly than anything
else. I think it is really this that Winters has found
in Laforgue, and that enables him to say of *Ulysses*
that "It is adolescent as Laforgue is adolescent; it is
ironic about feelings which are not worth the irony." [31]
Yet his failure to take account of tone in his comparison between Marvell and Herrick leads to a reading of

the two poems in which the nature of the feeling in
each is confused and misread, and which results in a
disastrously wrong relative judgment.

4

It is often difficult to escape the feeling that
Winters considers a poem defective not because the
emotion is in excess of the theme, but because it is in
excess of the paraphrasable content—which is very
likely no more than the ghost of the theme. His
treatment of Hopkins must be counted, in this respect,
especially severe. The essay [32] is perhaps the first *serious*
consideration of Hopkins from a hostile point of view,
and any future reading of Hopkins will have to take it
into account. I think that Winters' choice of poems
for discussion could have been more happily made.
But the essay is so interesting, both in itself and in
relation to Winters' general theory of poetry, that it
deserves to be looked at in some detail, particularly as
Hopkins is one of the few poets whose work Winters
has analyzed at length in print.

With some of the poems Winters seems to have had
unnecessary difficulty: his reading occasionally appears
tired and careless, as if he weren't really interested.
Thus of *Duns Scotus's Oxford* he writes that it "offers
an octet devoted to a description of the Oxford land-
scape, with especial reference to the mingling of city
and country and the regrettable domination of the
city." [33] The poem is, I think, one of Hopkins's least
interesting, but it doesn't deserve this kind of casual
treatment. Thus: to *encounter* is not to mingle
(though the city is "branchy between towers"). And
the second quatrain of the octet refers not to the
regrettable domination of the city, but to the spoiling
by a "graceless growth," "a base and brickish skirt" (as
opposed to the stone of the real city) that "sours that
neighbour-nature thy grey beauty is grounded best in,"

of the intimate union between real city and real country. This part of the poem is an early attack on subtopia; and perhaps Winters (who is reputed to have crossed the Rockies only once) can hardly be blamed for not knowing in detail the effects of suburbanization on the relation between town and country in England; possibly as an American he could hardly understand the change. But he doesn't seem to have even attended to what the poem says.

There are other cases of misreading on more important issues, mainly because poems don't behave in exactly the way Winters expects them to. I feel that at times he has made no attempt to see whether there is any substance beneath the imagery. That Hopkins's imagery is loose is a charge Winters often brings – and, when he goes into detail, with much justification. His discussion of *The Windhover* contains the observation that "To describe a bird, however beautifully, and to imply that Christ is like him but greater, is to do very little toward indicating the greatness of Christ." [34] Perhaps it would be unreasonable to ask Winters what *might* be a suitable way of indicating the greatness of Christ, since he has himself confessed that he is probably constitutionally incapable of becoming a Christian. In any case I think the point is just with regard to a number of the poems, in which Hopkins begins with an octet of more or less pure "nature-poetry" and follows with a sextet putting in an explicit and lame moral. Of the bird in *The Windhover*, Winters goes on "His image resembles the image of the anvil in *No worst, there is none*, in which we get the physical embodiment of the meaning, without the meaning, or with too small a part of it." [35]

I believe that Winters' account of the *Windhover* is substantially justified. The poem has been greatly overpraised, largely because of its obscurity, and the attractions of its romantic description.[36] Winters is able to demonstrate very effectively that the relation asserted between its two parts simply isn't realized within the poem. In other cases, however, we find him using less his own powers of analysis than the expectations which he brings from a reading of quite different poets. Of *God's Grandeur* he writes,

> The first line offers a major concept, in impressive phrasing. Instead of developing the concept, as a concept, however, in the manner of a poet of the Renaissance, Hopkins proceeds to illustrate it with two descriptive figures.[37]

Again, I think that Winters justifies his stricture on this poem. It is the invocation of the poet of the Renaissance which is disturbing. His methods have become the rule for all to follow, and his presence here suggests that Winters is simply not going to consider seriously any poetry which departs substantially from this norm of "developing concepts as concepts." Winters would say that this is the only rational thing to do with concepts, but it isn't, for example, always Shakespeare's way.[38]

We meet the Renaissance poet again in connexion with *The Starlight Night*, where we learn that "A devotional poet of the Renaissance, dealing with 'prayer, patience, alms, vows,' would have had a good deal to say of each." [39] He is also perhaps responsible for Winters' somewhat doctrinaire approach to scansion. Winters' metrical markings are sometimes an improvement on Hopkins's own; but his insistence on the overriding importance of scansion in terms of feet rather than accent makes for strained readings and leads him to give up some lines altogether. He is never content to let the verse dictate its own movement but must impose a metrical system upon it. This leads to some readings, whose variation from those that the natural rhythm of the English words seems to insist on, are too large to be accounted for by transatlantic differences of pronunciation. Of Wordsworth's *Westminster Bridge* he writes:

> an extremely smooth iambic movement has been established in the first five lines, so effectively established that it dominates the sixth line, and almost any reader who is aware of rhythm at all will be forced to impose a very light iambic emphasis on the first two feet of the sixth line; to do otherwise will bring the poem apart in ruins.[40]

As far as my own ear will judge, this account produces a complete travesty of the movement of the poem, which I find nearly as varied, both in speed and in accent, as it could well be if the iambic foot is to be felt at all. The sixth line, unquestionably, is the most extreme variant in the poem from the standard pentameter; it slows the movement as much as can be borne, and to read it as Winters says it should be read produces a fantastic effect. What has happened in this case is another triumph of theory over experience. Theory (which has admittedly been generalized from experience of Renaissance poets) lays down certain conditions for the occurrence of a spondaic foot. These conditions not being fulfilled in Wordsworth's case, the first four syllables of the line must be read as two iambs, "in spite of everything" (as Winters says), including the affront that it offers to the movement of the poem, to the natural form of the words, and to the sense of the line as a whole. Thus is the scholar's ear rule-bound.

To return to Hopkins: Winters' devotion to Renaissance ideals is doubtless responsible for his cavalier dismissal of so many of Hopkins's poems. Everywhere, Winters finds

> emotional intensity for its own sake, metrical elaboration for its own sake, metaphor for its own sake, repetition and elaboration of structure for their own sake. The

poem becomes at once an unrestrained indulgence in meaningless emotion, and an unrestrained exercise in meaningless ingenuity; the poet has no responsibility to understand and evaluate his subject truly. If one will consider such poems as *The Wreck of the Deutschland, The Loss of the Eurydice, Binsey Poplars, Spelt from Sibyl's Leaves,* and *The Leaden Echo and the Golden Echo,* to mention only some of the more obvious examples, one will find the perfect product of the theory. The paraphrasable content of all these poems is so slight as to be reducible to a sentence or two for each. The structures erected upon these simple bases are so fantastically elaborate that the subjects are all but lost and the poems frequently verge upon the ludicrous.[41]

Certainly Hopkins does provide examples of emotional intensity displayed for its own sake, but I find the list included in this paragraph a singular one. And I suggest that the man, who will say of *Spelt from Sibyl's Leaves* that the metrical elaboration, repetition, etc., are there for their own sake, is simply not prepared to consider whether there are not other ways of using language than the one he is used to. Winters nowhere examines any of these poems in detail, so that it seems irrelevant here to propose a defence. But the passage is worth noting as another illustration of the dangers likely to arise when too much reliance is placed on ability to extract the "paraphrasable content" of poems like these.

One of the most interesting parts of this essay contains an elaborate discussion of *No worst, there is none,* which is compared with poems by Donne (*Thou hast made me*) and by Bridges (*Low Barometer*). The comparison is very unfavourable to Hopkins, though Winters' strictures on his poem are in the main just. But his condemnation depends on his being able to provide a positive account of the other two poems, and this can only be done if one is very casual about the nature of Bridges' use of language. So Winters is able to ignore manifest weaknesses: having apparently convinced himself of the dignity of the conceptual thought which lies behind the poem, he has gone on to assume that the poem itself has an equal dignity. But this is to substitute something else for what the poem is. We have here an interesting case of a poem on an entirely generalized theme, not professing (as Winters says) to deal with a personal experience, a poem in which the critic takes for granted that an adequate motive has been provided. Yet an examination of the language leads me to ask if anything has been grasped at all. The "ancient and powerful demonic forces" exist only in more or less meaningless asbtractions (like "squalid lease of sin"), so that one is forced to ask, "What is Bridges talking about?" Winters claims to know exactly, but there is very little evidence from the poem that Bridges knew. And I can't see that Winters has established any good grounds, even on his own terms, for preferring the poem to Hopkins's, save that the violence here is apparently attached to something general; there is probably as much uncertainty in each of them.

5

In discussing this poem of Bridges, Winters seems to have paid nothing like enough attention to the quality of the language in which the poet's experience is realized. This is a serious fault in one who believes that the superiority of the short poem lies in its power to pack experiences into small limits and thus make the conveyance, the generalization, of the experience more powerful. Early in *Primitivism and Decadence*, in fact, Winters offers a paragraph in which he gives an account of the virtues of poetry which might seem to fit very well some poets whom he appears to think least of:

> a poem in the first place should offer us new perceptions, not only of the exterior universe, but of human experience as well; it should add, in other words, to what we have already seen. This is the elementary function for the reader. The corresponding function for the poet is a sharpening and training of his sensibilities; the very exigencies of the medium as he employs it in the act of perception should force him to the discovery of values which he never would have found without the convening of all the conditions of that particular act, conditions one or more of which will be the necessity of solving some particular difficulty such as the location of a rhyme or the perfection of a cadence without disturbance to the remainder of the poem. The poet who suffers from such difficulties instead of profiting by them is only in a rather rough sense a poet at all.
>
> If, however, the difficulties of versification are a stimulant merely to the *poet*, the reader may argue that he finds them a hindrance to himself and that he prefers some writer of prose who appears to offer him as much with less trouble to all concerned. The answer to such a reader is that the appearance of equal richness in the writer of prose is necessarily deceptive.
>
> For language is a kind of abstraction, even at its most concrete; such a word as "cat," for instance, is generic and not particular. Such a word becomes particular only in so far as it gets into some kind of experiential complex, which qualifies it and limits it, which gives it, in short, a local habitation as well as a name. Such a complex is the poetic line or other unit, which, in turn, shoud be a functioning part of the larger complex, or poem.[42]

On the whole there is little to quarrel with in this passage. As an account of the kind and degree of attention involved in both the writing and the reading of poetry it seems convincing. Presumably Winters would say that Hopkins is one of the poets who suffers from the difficulties mentioned rather than one who profits by them. So at times he does. But at this level Bridges hardly begins to be a poet even in a rough sense. For he does not give us new perceptions; there is no sense of his being forced to the discovery of new values through the strain of locating a rhyme or perfecting a cadence. And indeed in this very phrase is the one main danger signal that the passage offers. I think it would be a rather loosely constructed poem (perhaps a poem "only in a rather rough sense") which could be polished in the way Winters implies without *disturbance* to the rest of the poem. If in the location of a rhyme or the perfection of a cadence the poet is forced to the discovery of new values, then this discovery cannot leave the remainder of the poem "undisturbed," if the justice of the poet's evaluation is to persist into the least important syllable. It is exactly this kind of "disturbance" which gives the poem its genuineness and its life, making it a live experience for the poet and reader instead of a dead exercise in locating rhymes. But Winters consistently underestimates the capacity of what Leavis calls the poetic-creative use of language to realize and define fresh levels of experience, new values. He clearly prefers the poetry of straightforward statement and is here sometimes inclined to take the will for the deed.

Rhymes and cadences are aspects of style, of the technique through which an experience is realized: they qualify the "form" of a poem. Now there is perhaps rather too much talk about "form" in Winters, though I agree roughly with his conception of what "form" is:

> the poet, in striving toward an ideal of poetic form at which he has arrived through the study of other poets, is

actually striving to perfect a moral attitude toward that range of experience of which he is aware.[43]

An "ideal of poetic form" is not perhaps something that a poet should consciously strive towards: for Winters writes as if it is external and antecedent to each poem. So elsewhere he has remarked on the virtues of the poet's formulating valid critical principles.[44] I should suppose that the poet, striving to evaluate and shape his experience, is creating his "ideal of form" afresh in each poem. The sharpening and training of sensibility should not issue in an ideal and unvarying formula. But Winters does see clearly that in the well-conceived poem "form" expresses the poet's attitude. Consequently he is particularly severe on formlessness whenever he meets (or thinks he meets) it.

Form is expressive invariably of the state of mind of the author: a state of formlessness is legitimate subject matter for literature, and in fact all subject matter, as such, is relatively formless; but the author must endeavor to give form, or meaning, to the formless—in so far as he endeavors that his own state of mind may imitate or approximate the condition of the matter, he is surrendering to the matter instead of mastering it. Form, in so far as it endeavors to imitate the formless, destroys itself.[45]

Subject-matter is formless at a point before any judgment—any perception—of it has occurred. In this sense the crudest decision imposes form in some degree. Moreover, all merely descriptive statements do, as Winters has said, govern the general possibilities of feeling derivable from the matter. But general possibilities are not enough; and Winters is certainly right when he insists that

To say that a poet is justified in employing a disintegrating form in order to express a feeling of disintegration, is merely a sophisticatical justification of bad poetry, akin to the Whitmanian notion that one must write loose and sprawling poetry to "express" the loose and sprawling American continent.[46]

The conception of form as the shaping of experience enables Winters to say that "In so far as form is enfeebled, precision of detail is enfeebled, . . . to say that detail is enfeebled is to say that the power of discrimination is enfeebled." [47] Such an attitude has, I believe, enabled Winters to make some very telling criticism of Joyce, and it is a stick used to beat Eliot with great earnestness. A specific comparison is made between him and Baudelaire, as poets both dealing with society deprived of grace and prone to the sin of acedia, but "Eliot surrenders his form to his subject, whereas Baudelaire does not." [48]

Whatever one thinks of such particular judgments, it is through Winters' understanding of form that he is able to penetrate to the heart of the disease which he calls romanticism, in which there is a special concentration on "feeling" at the expense of a properly motivating situation. Thus, writing of Frost, he observes:

> Frost's instinctualism, his nostalgia for dream and chaos, are merely the symptoms of sentimental obscurantism when, as in Frost's work, they are dealt with lightly and whimsically, but if taken seriously, as in the work of Crane and Pound, they may lead to more serious difficulties. They do not lead toward intelligence, no matter how far the individual devotee may travel in their company; they lead away from intelligence. They lead away from the true comprehension of human experience which makes for great, or even for successful, poetry.[49]

Winters' dislike of "romanticism," of the excess of emotion beyond any presented situation, and his distrust of obscurity are undoubtedly healthy. They are essentially linked with his rationalism, yet they are perhaps to be seen as the good side of an attitude which unfortunately also prevents his appreciating the nature of the poetic-creative use of language.[50] Initially it might seem here as if his principles are sound but his own judgment not sensitive enough. But this is to make too sharp a distinction. For his principles have deeply affected his habits of perception. The effect of this can be seen in the curious and superficial distinction that he makes between "traditional" and "experimental" poetry.

> *Traditional poetry* is poetry which endeavors to utilize the greatest possible amount of the knowledge and wisdom, both technical and moral, but technical only in so far as it does not obstruct the moral, to be found in precedent poetry. It assumes the ideal existence of a normal quality of feeling, a normal convention, to which the convention of any particular poem should more or less conform. . . . One might describe it [the traditional norm] negatively as that type of poetry which displays at one and the same time the greatest possible distinction with the fewest possible characteristics recognizable as the marks of any particular school, period, or man; as, in brief, that type of poetry which displays the greatest polish of style and the smallest trace of mannerism. . . .
>
> *Experimental poetry* endeavors to widen the racial experience, or to alter it, or to get away from it, by establishing abnormal conventions. In one sense or another Spenser, Donne, Milton, Hopkins, Laforgue, and Rimbaud are experimental poets of a very marked kind. The most striking example in English of a convention of heightened intensity (that is, of what the unsympathetic might call poetic strain) is to be found in *Paradise Lost*. . . . As an act of invention, of daring experiment, the creation of Miltonic blank verse, both meter and rhetoric, is not equaled in English poetry; in fact one is

tempted to wonder if it is equaled in any other. . . . Yet in spite of his mastery, the emphatic and violent rhetoric which he created limits his range, as compared to the range of Shakespeare, a man of comparable genius but working in a series of conventions which are relatively traditional. . . . Milton is the more complex rhetorician, but the simpler moralist and a man of far less subtle perception. Milton is the nobler, but Milton's nobility is in part, and as compared to Shakespeare, the over-emphasis of imperception.[51]

The contrast which Winters offers here is much too sharp and much too simple. There is no one *normal* way to write poetry, and all conventions must have been "abnormal" at some time in the sense merely that they were new. Every major poet extends the possibilities of language in some way or other, through the pressure of original experience demanding expression. Shakespeare did more than any other English poet has ever done to enlarge the language, though—his coinages notwithstanding—it would be wrong to see this as a deliberate act of invention. Most of the poets Winters describes as experimental did no doubt make inventions—the most extreme so far made in English is surely Joyce's *Finnegans Wake*. It may be that these poets, with their extreme innovations have in fact done less to refresh and broaden the language than those who extend the range of an existing tradition. But tradition is not a narrow and permanent *restriction* of possibilities; it exists only in the poets who can use the language as a living medium, to be made new in every generation. In fact, nothing works so against a continuing live tradition as the poet who merely lives among past forms (though he may derogatorily and inaccurately be called "traditional"). Some "inventions" do enlarge tradition and so help to keep it living: others are too far from the character of the language at the stage it has reached and too violently distort it to really extend our range of thought and expression. In such cases there is always the possibility (surely a certainty in Joyce's) that the invention has in reality been made for its own sake rather than from the pressure of new experience. Winters *seems* to argue that it was simply because he worked in traditional conventions that Shakespeare is a man of far more subtle perception than Milton. But Shakespeare just is a man of far more subtle perception; and he found more new ways of expression to meet this than Milton did, even if the process was less spectacular. Shakespeare's perception could not have found expression in Milton's language—not because Milton's language is too experimental, but because it is too limited, permitting only certain specialized lines of thought and feeling. Milton aimed not at extending the possibilities of expression but at limiting them (though in a new way) and thus settling thought and experience in a certain more or less fixed direction. Consequently his contribution to the growth of the language has been a blind alley, though one which has had unhappy and large-scale effects on our later literature.[52]

I take it that the qualification in Winters' first sentence—"technical only in so far as it does not obstruct the moral"—*is* an admission that the techniques of earlier poets are not necessarily adaptable by their successors, since technique is only determined by experience. At the same time I see no a priori reason why it should be a special virtue for technique to be invisible, for it is the expression of character. It is obvious enough that Winters thinks that traditional poetry is inherently superior to experimental. So there must be great and special merit in the absence of recognizable marks. But these, where they exist, need not be mannerisms—they may, after all, be the marks of style, which is to say character.

6

At the centre of Winters' theory of poetry is his view that literature must communicate not only an experience but a valuable attitude to it. The poem will be a judgment of experience, and the more significant the experience and the more accurate and profound the judgment, the greater the value of the poem in "enriching human experience," and the greater its ability to "increase the intelligence and strengthen the moral temper." This relating of literature to the whole field of human experience seems to me the essential first part of an answer to the question raised in the chapter dealing with Burke: although one cannot live on art and must have experiences simply of living, there are times when an experience of art is preferred, when one would rather go to a tragedy even if it means breaking a date: how does this come about? Winters' answer seems to me incomplete partly because he restricts his discussion to our experience of individual works of art alone, partly because his stiffly rational approach makes the relation between the poem and its original generating experience too explicit and too simple. The first of these aspects leads to the argument of my next chapter; the second deserves a little more discussion here.

At one point in his long attack on Eliot's theories and methods, Winters asks himself the question, "what, after all, is a poem, if we approach it in my own innocent state of mind?" [53] His answer is much as we should expect, but it has one puzzling aspect:

> It is a statement about an experience, real or imag-
> ined. The statement must follow the experience in time:
> Donne, for example, could not have written *The Ecstasy*
> while engaged in the experience described. The poem is
> a commentary upon something that has happened or
> that has been imagined as having happened; it is an act

of meditation. The poem is more valuable than the event by virtue of its being an act of meditation: it is the event plus the understanding of the event.[54]

Now why should the poem necessarily be more valuable than the event? Not all acts of meditation are valuable; it depends on the event and on the poem. For in one very obvious sense the event (say that described in *The Ecstasy*) is *not* included within the poem: and even the most faithful report of it may have less value just because it is not the real thing, or again it *may* have more.[55]

Winters writes as if the two things—event and understanding—stood side by side in the poem; it is noticeable that the poems which he explicitly prefers are those in which the two *are* fairly well marked off from one another. Poems which, he claims, give "the illusion of the immediate experience without intervention of understanding" he condemns very severely (Eliot is the chief object of his scorn). And I think that this "illusion" is the real obstacle for him in the way of a proper understanding of the working of drama. He does—for all his rejection of it—often approach didacticism, asking for the moral comment to be explicit and is at sea where something subtler is being offered. So he regrets that

Jonson, like Shakespeare, is handicapped by the mimetic principle: Dryden was able to depict Shadwell in Dryden's language and to relate him directly to Dryden's principles; Jonson was forced to depict Volpone in Volpone's language and with relation to Volpone's principles. Jonson did a remarkably brilliant piece of work, if one considers the limitations of his medium, but Dryden did a better—it would not be hard to devise a very good argument to the effect that Dryden's Shadwell, as we get him in *MacFlecknoe* and in the portrait of Og in the second part of *Absalom and Achitophel*, is the greatest comic figure in our literature. Yet Jonson was a far greater poet than Dryden; the evidence lies elsewhere.[56]

Now I find this an almost exact reversal of the truth. I think that Dryden did do a remarkably brilliant piece of work but that Jonson did a better: and I think that in this the "mimetic principle" helped him greatly. For (innocently enough) I should have supposed that it is just because Volpone condemns himself out of his own mouth that Jonson's presentation of him is so effective. Certainly Volpone is seen in relation to Volpone's principles; but more—Volpone's principles are seen in relation to Jonson's. Surely the opening speech of the play (which Winters refers to) is an example of just how penetrating and forceful the moral judgment of a play can be, exactly because it refrains from explicit comment.[57]

The likeness one may feel here to the limitations of another "moralistic" critic—Johnson—is suggested also by Winters' announcement that "A sound attitude toward a major problem, communicated with adequacy of detail, is what we ordinarily mean by sublimity."[58] This is very dignified. No doubt many speeches in the House of Commons are sublime; but Winters' statement is absurd if he really is trying to describe ordinary usage. Furthermore, it involves him in some very odd assertions when he employs it. For example "A Bach fugue or a Byrd mass moves us not primarily because of any originality it may display, but because of its sublimity as I have already defined the term."[59] I have no idea what are the major problems that Winters would be referring to here. But it is in any case unnecessary to move outside literature to realize the limited usefulness of bringing in this conception of sublimity. The range of major problems and sound attitudes which can be isolated in Winters' way will be exhausted fairly quickly, leaving a lot of the moral substance of art behind. Winters is a remarkably brilliant and intelligent critic, and in particular he asks many of the right questions. But the limitations of his moralism, to some extent forced on him by the formulations which he has deliberately selected, prevent his being able to give sufficiently comprehensive answers, so that he allows poetry to do greatly less than it can.

Johnson cannot understand that works of art *enact* their moral valuations. It is not enough that Shakespeare, on the evidence of his works, "thinks" (and feels), morally; for Johnson a moral judgment that isn't *stated* isn't there. Further, he demands that the whole play shall be conceived and composed as statement. The dramatist must start with a conscious and abstractly formulated moral and proceed to manipulate his puppets so as to demonstrate and enforce it.[1]

The charge that Leavis makes here could be turned on Winters almost unchanged. It would not be quite accurate to accuse Winters of insisting on *statements* of moral judgment: statements there must be, but the moral comment comes for him more in the fitness of the accompanying emotion. Yet his treatment of drama has the disabilities that Leavis notes here in Johnson, and it would be fair to say of him that

he cannot appreciate the life-principle of drama as we have it in the poetic-creative use of language—the use by which the stuff of experience is presented to speak and act for itself.[2]

Winters is far too prone to write as if the "event" and the understanding—the judgment—of it stand side by side. One result is (paradoxically) that he overestimates poems in which the situation, the stimulus of the poet's emotional response, is not present in the work itself, but either simply taken for granted or at best given a bare acknowledgment to which the emotion is attached without being essentially rooted in it.

This is perhaps the largest issue of critical principle which separates Winters from Leavis. But for Leavis the "principle," the stress on *enactment*, on the presence of the "stuff of experience" speaking for itself in the poem, is no merely asserted dogma: the poetic-creative use of language, creating both new possibilities of experience and a new sense of relative values, is for him the crux: this is what gives paramount significance to literature. The fusion of situation, response, and expression is the sign of a poet genuinely alive to his own experience, and it is the guarantee of the relevance and validity of his presentment of it for the world in general.

The point which perhaps needs greatest emphasis in the approach to Leavis' criticism is that the terms he regularly uses in his analysis, the closeness to the words, imagery and movement of a poem of that analysis itself, his insistence always on working in terms of concrete judgments—these are not things pursued for their own sake, or as the dogmas of "practical criticism" but relate essentially to his effort to assess the human significance of the work for its readers and in the whole contemporary situation in which it exists at any given time. A particularly good illustration is the fascinating exercise in comparative analysis called "Reality and Sincerity." [3] For my present purposes the most relevant part of this essay is the demonstration of the superiority of Hardy's *After a Journey* to Emily Brontë's *Remembrance*. This demonstration is itself a lengthy analysis of Hardy's poem (with cross references to Emily Brontë's)—much too long to quote in full. The opening passage, however illustrates the method of analysis to be used, the larger criteria by which the poems will be judged, and the justification of the first as settling the degree to which each poem answers the second.

A difference in manner and tone between Hardy's poem and the other two will have been observed at once: unlike them it is not declamatory. The point should in justice lead on to a positive formulation, and this may not come as readily; certain stylistic characteristics that may at first strike the reader as oddities and clumsinesses tend to delay the recognition of the convincing intimate naturalness. It turns out, however, that the essential ethos of the manner is given in

> *Where you will next be there is no knowing.* . . .

This intimacy we are at first inclined to describe as 'conversational,' only to replace that adjective by 'self-communing' when we have recognized that, even when Hardy (and it is significant that we say 'Hardy') addresses the 'ghost' he is still addressing himself. And it shouldn't take long to recognize that the marked idiosyncracy of idiom and diction going with the intimacy of tone achieves some striking precisions and felicities. Consider, for instance the verb in

> *Facing round about me everywhere.* . . .

There is nothing that strikes us as odd in that 'facing,' but it is a use created for the occasion, and when we look into its unobtrusive naturalness it turns out to have a positive and 'inevitable' rightness, the analysis of which involves a precise account of the 'ghost's' status—which in its turn involves a precise account of the highly specific situation defined by the poem.

Then again, there is that noun in the fourth line which (I can testify) has offended readers not incapable of recognizing its felicity:

> *And the unseen waters' ejaculations awe me.*

'Ejaculations' gives with vivid precision the sound that 'awes' Hardy: the slap of the waves on the rocky walls; the slap with its prolonging reverberant syllables—the hollow voice, in fact, that, in stanza three, 'seems to call out to me from forty years ago' (and the hollowness rings significantly through the poem).

In fact, the difference first presenting itself as an absence of declamatory manner and tone, examined, leads to the perception of positive characteristics—precisions of concrete realization, specificities, complexities —that justify the judgement I now advance: Hardy's poem, put side by side with Emily Brontë's, is seen to have a great advantage in *reality*. This term, of course, has to be given its due force by the analysis yet to be done—the analysis it sums up; but it provides the right pointer. And to invoke another term, more inescapably one to which a critic must try and give some useful force by appropriate and careful use, if he can contrive that: to say that Hardy's poem has an advantage in reality is to say (it will turn out) that it represents a profounder and completer sincerity.[4]

Most of the rest of the essay is an elaboration and justification of the generalizations set out here. What I want to emphasize are the criteria invoked in the discrimination that Leavis makes. His stress falls first on Hardy's "great advantage in reality": the instances included in this passage show something of the way in which Hardy uses language to convey the special quality of the particular experience which—we cannot doubt—he has undergone: *this* experience, not another one, and an experience of himself in such and such a *given* situation. The point is in the "given"—the fact that Hardy gives us not only his response but the occasion and the experience that move him (it is significant that we cannot, in fact, separate the three, for the experience is only fully created within the poem). Through looking at Hardy's particularities of

utterance, the varied movement of the verse, the precise and vivid *seeing* of the ghost, while it yet remains a
ghost, recognizing a hint of wry irony in the way Hardy
looks at himself, which gives a nice detachment, an
ability to see himself without reducing our sense of
how deep the loss is: in these ways we approach and
comprehend the delicate question of Hardy's own
position in the poem, and we come to a decision about
his seriousness, his sincerity, we make a judgment
about the worth of the poem as we experience it, its
worth as an experience to us and as a possible
influence—however slight—on our future ways of
thought and feeling.

The analysis, of course, has not yet been carried out.
When it has been, the result is to amplify our sense of
the "reality" of Hardy's poem and at the same time to
justify the near-identification of this quality with his
sincerity. "Sincerity" is not always a useful term in
literary criticism: its relevance depends to some extent
on the kind of work being discussed, and I shall later
quote another argument of Leavis' in terms of "reality" which rightly does not involve the second word at
all. Yet in this poem we recognize that the two qualities are inseparable: the experience cannot even be
identified without this precise expression, and this is
the short statement of what makes it so fundamentally
superior to Emily Brontë's. For in her poem there is no
precise delineation; and we therefore suspect not so
much the quality of the experience as its nature, if
indeed it was there at all.

I am assuming, of course, that the experience, once
we are in a position to grasp it ourselves, does in fact
have real value for us. This is not itself guaranteed by a
poem's sincerity, for the experience may be trifling. I
don't think that anyone has suggested *this* of Hardy's
poem; but different habits of reading may, even in the

face of so detailed an analysis, make for serious differences in judgment. Leavis' conclusion is that Hardy's honesty in facing and giving his experience for what it really is involves a final "affirmation," a positive acceptance of *life*:

> Not to take the significance of that 'Trust me, I mind not' is to have failed to respond to the complexity of the total attitude, and to have failed to realize the rare kind of integrity the poem achieves. It is to miss the suggestion of paradoxical insistence, the intensity of directed feeling and will, in 'Nay, bring me here again.' For what in the bringing of him here, he may be supposed to mind is not the arduousness, for an old man, of the long journey and the ramble by night. 'To bring me here,' says Hardy, 'is to make me experience to the full the desolation and the pang—to give a sharp edge to the fact of Time's derision. But I don't mind—I more than don't mind: bring me here again! I hold to life, even though life as a total fact lours. The *real* for me, the focus of my affirmation, is the remembered realest thing, though to remember vividly is at the same time, inescapably, to embrace the utterness of loss.' [5]

Vincent Buckley on the other hand, sees this account as Leavis' own rewriting of Hardy's intentions. Agreeing that there is something affirmative about the poem he nonetheless doesn't find this to have great substance:

> The 'ethos with which the poem leaves us at the end' is not simply one which the working of the poem itself has established, it implies an ultimate attitude to life. That attitude, on its philosophical side, is a sort of stoicism in a minor key; while its moral expression is a kind of courage. These qualities no doubt give evidence of a 'rare kind of integrity.' But do they result in a great poem? Certainly they do not express an affirmation of life of anything like the intensity and completeness of, say, Yeats' 'Sailing to Byzantium,' or Marvell's 'Hora-

tian Ode'—poems which are very different from each other in affirmation, but both clearly great. It seems to me that the very specificity of reference which is so appropriate to it, and which Leavis counts on so much, are actually in this case a barrier to greatness.[6]

The intention of Buckley's first sentence seems to be to assert that this particular "ultimate attitude" at least is one adopted outside of any single experience. What he understands by an ultimate attitude to life reveals itself in the sentence which follows as a philosophical position which can be more or less adequately defined in general terms, can be shared by any number of people, and can be expected to be illustrated in the reported experiences of individuals. I suggest that Buckley has not merely failed to find the stoicism worked out in the poem: he has in fact brought it with him (though I do not know at all what he means by the minor key). We should naturally expect so deeply felt a poem to accord in some way with what else we know of Hardy; and it is usually held to be a commonplace that Hardy's "ultimate attitude to life" can be summed up as "stoicism." Yet there is very little of stoicism or of the characteristic pessimism of most of Hardy's fiction in this poem; and the "kind of courage" is a rare kind indeed.

Buckley has accused Leavis of rewriting Hardy's intentions, of finding in the poem what he wanted to find; yet Buckley himself has evidently brought to it expectations of a particular kind which have stood in the way of his finding in the poem the real experience it has to give. The two poems which he brings in to compare with Hardy's are indeed very different from one another, but they share one characteristic which Hardy's lacks, in that the themes of both are explicitly generalized within the poems. Yeats's poem, one might almost say, is conceived as an illustration of a general (an "ultimate") attitude: it is more than this description suggests, because the language is creative enough to make us aware that Yeats is himself directly experiencing this attitude as something living for him. And Marvell, taking like Hardy a particular event (or rather series of events), differs from him in that these are already in a sense public property before they are realized afresh in the poem; as the poem proceeds Marvell develops a complex attitude toward the events and what they stand for, and as he is so sensitive to their wide human implications, the poem grows in value through the real importance and representativeness of the events themselves. But an event does not necessarily become important just by being public property. Most events which are, or can be, public property in this sense are entirely trivial. Buckley has, I feel, started with the attitude that publicness of subject gives a poem a head start over one in which the experience which lies at its heart is an essentially personal one. This at any rate seems to be implied by the last sentence of the quotation. For it is the specificity of reference in Hardy's poem which makes the experience so alive for the reader, setting it down in all its own particular qualities and distinguishing it from all others. And evidently Buckley feels that no "ultimate attitude" can be contained or worked out within the expression of one given experience. (Possibly he is right, and we shouldn't be looking for ultimate attitudes: they sound like the sort of thing which turns out to be ultimately dead.) So he pins Hardy down to his "stoicism" and then lectures him.

Now it is true that *After a Journey* has a special personal flavour. Yet to recreate the personal experience within the poem is to make it public in the sense that it can now be shared. It does not cease to be a personal experience, but if the poem is successful it

becomes something more, and by this time the distinction between private and public becomes empty. We
do not, I think, feel any inclination to generalize the
experience in Hardy's poem, to say that such-and-such
an attitude is what we should take to sorrow or loss in
general. But as we register Hardy's own particular
reactions and attitudes, noting the deliberateness of
his re-entry and of his acceptance of the whole situation for him, we may find such a general word as
"courage" or "integrity" useful as a pointer:
("buoyancy" is what seems to me above all to characterize the poem's close—a buoyancy without the least
trace of heartiness or shallow optimism but very far
removed from stoicism or resignation). And without
meeting anything in the nature of a social tone or
social references in the poem, we may recognize that
the ease and naturalness of Hardy's characteristic
manner implicitly make felt the social world in which
it is natural to express this kind of loyalty and affec-
tion. It is difficult to see how a poem which can affect
the reader so directly and poignantly could invoke an
"ultimate attitude" in any more satisfying way.

I have spent some time on this example, because it
shows particularly clearly Leavis' stress on the importance of seeing and judging what is *in* a poem
("something that should contain within itself the
reason why it is so and not otherwise") and also a
significant illustration, in Buckley's reaction, of the
danger of importing things of one's own.[7] And it shows
equally clearly the way in which a study by the means
of "practical criticism," the close examination and
analysis of words, of imagery, of movement, leads to
the centre of his work, which is the discovery and
demonstration of the nature and quality of the experience which is brought to life in the texture of words. So
we find Leavis over and over again implicating, in one
direction or the other, the close relation between ex-

pression and the experience which gives rise to it; and the emphasis on "the words on the page" always has a specific end in view—to make clear some aspect of the life engaged in (or missing from) the poem. To cite two negative examples, Leavis remarks of Tennyson's *Tears, Idle Tears* that its particularity reveals no justifying situation for the emotion, and that "no new definitions or directions of feeling derive from . . . [its] suggestions of imagery." [8] And more generally he says that "a weakness of realization . . . affects the poet's grasp of his themes, conceptions and interests."[9]

Now just as, I have suggested, there seems no good reason for trying to generalize the experience in Hardy's poem, so the character of Leavis' interest in it remains closely defined by character of the experience itself. It is a sign of the closeness of Leavis' criticism to the work in hand, his disinclination to indulge in the larger critical or subcritical gestures, that to make, as René Wellek would have him do, a philosophy out of his choices, preferences, and convictions is peculiarly difficult, and (I think Leavis is right here) largely irrelevant for the literary critic. But I shall quote here another passage of some length to try to draw out something of the particular kind of "interest in man, society and civilization" that Leavis brings to bear on literature. The passage is part of a discussion in which Leavis illustrates the special impressiveness of George Eliot's Gwendolen Harleth through a comparison with James's Isabel Archer.

> The point [of comparing the two] is to bring out the force of James's own tribute (paid through Constantius) to the characteristic strength of George Eliot's art as exhibited in her protagonist:
>
> > And see how the girl is known, inside out, how thoroughly she is felt and understood. It is the most *in-*

telligent thing in all George Eliot's writing; and that is saying much. It is so deep, so true, so complete, it holds such a wealth of psychological detail, it is more than masterly.

It would hardly be said of Isabel Archer that the presentment of her is complete; it is characteristic of James's art to have made her an effective enough presence for his purpose without anything approaching a 'wealth of psychological detail.' Her peculiar kind of impressiveness, in fact, is conditioned by her *not* being known inside out, and—we have to confess it—could *not* have been achieved by George Eliot: she knows too much about that kind of girl. For it is fair to say that if James had met a Gwendolen Harleth (at any rate, an American one) he would have seen Isabel Archer; he immensely admired George Eliot's inwardness and completeness of rendering, but when he met the type in actual life and was prompted to the conception of *The Portrait of a Lady*, he saw her with the eyes of an American gentleman. One must add—an essential point—that he saw *her* as American.

It is, of course, possible to imagine a beautiful, clever and vital girl, with 'that sense of superior claims which made a large part of her consciousness' (George Eliot's phrase for Gwendolen, but it applies equally to Isabel), whose egoism yet shouldn't be as much open to the criticism of an intelligent woman as Gwendolen's. But it is hard to believe that, in life, she could be as free from qualities inviting a critical response as the Isabel Archer seen by James. Asking of Gwendolen, why, though a mere girl, she should be everywhere a centre of deferential attention, George Eliot says (Chapter IV): 'The answer may seem to lie quite on the surface:—in her beauty, a certain unusualness about her, a decision of will which made itself felt in her graceful movements and clear unhesitating tones, so that if she came into the room on a rainy day when everybody else was flaccid and the use of things in general was not apparent to them, there seemed to be a sudden reason for keeping up the forms of life.' James might very well have been glad to have found these phrases for his heroine. But George Eliot isn't satisfied with the answer: she not only goes on, as James would hardly have done, to talk about the girl's 'inborn energy of egoistic desire,' she is very specific and concrete in exhibiting the play of that energy—the ways in which it imposes her claims on the people around her. And it is not enough to reply that James doesn't need to be specific to this effect—even granting, as we may, that the two authors are dealing with different girls: it is so plain that George Eliot knows more about hers than he about his, and that this accounts for an important part of the ostensible difference.

And in so far as the ostensible difference does, as we have to grant it does, go back to an actual difference in the object of the novelist's interest, then we must recognize, I think, that George Eliot's choice—one determined by the nature of her interests and the quality of her interestedness—of a Gwendolen rather than an Isabel is that of someone who knows and sees more and has a completer grasp of the real; and that it is one that enables the novelist to explore more thoroughly and profoundly the distinctive field of human nature, to be representative of which is the essential interest offered by both girls.[10]

I don't want to insist here on how far this particular relative placing is justified: my point is the criteria invoked. We see again a stress on the need not simply to talk about characteristics of the one girl or the other, but to be "very specific and concrete in exhibiting" them. But behind and informing this is a judgment on the function of each in her own novel, a judgment on what they stand for, on their relative success as explorations of "the distinctive field of human nature, to be representative of which is the essential interest offered by both girls." "George Eliot's choice . . . is that of someone who knows and sees more and has a completer grasp of the real." But what we have here is not a resurrection of "realism" in the nineteenth-century sense, though it has been taken for that. What we are after is the peculiar quality of the novelist's concern with life—not with the life of his characters as characters, but rather with what they stand for, with their function in a novel which is the exploration and working out of a rounded attitude to whole large stretches of our life. And George Eliot's "grasp of the real" is an understanding, a perception which is itself the working of moral judgment, involving already decisions, rejections, approvals, and preferences. George Eliot's selection—her decision to treat this aspect rather than that, to lay emphasis here and not there—shows already and inescapably the working of her moral imagination, which is then brought to a specific focus in detailed elaboration of character. So her "grasp of the real" depends on a technique at the opposite remove from that of a photograph; it is a matter of selective decisions, of saying that this and this are what really count, that that comes to show less relative significance, that such and such a particular view and judgment of an aspect of human nature is the one that compels itself on the observer. The great novelists, Leavis has said, "are significant in terms of the human awareness they promote; awareness of the possibilities of life." Correspondingly criticism, too, inescapably involves such moral judgments, which may sometimes seem to base themselves on criteria of humdrum realism: "it is hard to believe that, in life, she could be as free from qualities inviting a critical response as Isabel Archer seen by James." But the perception of how things are isn't just a necessary qualification for being aware of the "possibilities of

life"; in the greatest writers there can be no distinction: a perception of how things are is a judgment in
terms of possibilities understood and imaginatively
grasped.

If this is right, the photographic criterion of "realism" is beside the point: if we want to see the object
"as in itself it really is," no completely objective account of human relationships is possible, where "objective" is held to imply the withholding of moral
judgments, for a view without these is simply an inadequate and partial view. The effect of failing to see this
is interestingly illustrated in some remarks of Harold
Osborne as he discusses Leavis' view of James's late
novels. Writing in the following instance of *The
Golden Bowl*, Leavis makes abundantly clear that his
criticism implies a moral standpoint and a series of
moral judgments:

> What we are not reconciled to by any awareness of
> intentions is the outraging of our moral sense by the
> handling of the adultery theme—the triangle, or rather
> quadrilateral, of personal relations. We remain con-
> vinced that when an author, whatever symbolism he
> intends, presents a drama of men and women, he is
> committed to dealing in terms of men and women, and
> mustn't ask us to acquiesce in valuations that contradict
> our profoundest ethical sensibility. If, of course, he can
> work a revolutionary change in that sensibility, well and
> good, but who will contend that James's art in those late
> novels has that power? In *The Golden Bowl* we con-
> tinue to find our moral sense outraged.[11]

Osborne's view, however, is that this is not "moral
condemnation," by which he understands a condemnation of possible *influence*, not of perverse judgment:

> Dr. Leavis does not condemn James because he thinks
> that his influence on morals is bad. He is clear that these

novels can work no change in our moral views: indeed, if
they could revolutionize morality, Dr. Leavis's artistic
condemnation would be mitigated. He condemns them
simply because they are out of line with the moral views
which Dr. Leavis assumes his readers to share, and he
enunciates a general principle of criticism that any work
of literature which deals with men and women and
which contravenes accepted principles of morality must
be bad. This is in effect a condemnation on the basis of
inadequate Realism. What the critic says is that he is
unprepared to adopt the attitude of make-believe with
regard to any artistic presentation of moral views which
conflict notably with his own and that he proposes to
apply to them the same standards of judgment as he
would apply to similar views in the world of actuality.
He has failed in the aesthetic attitude or has, rather,
consciously refused to adopt the aesthetic attitude upon
this matter.[12]

This is a very remarkable account, but it may have
an appeal for those who do not immediately spot
Osborne's doubtless unconscious equivocation. The
statement is most obviously noteworthy for its use
(peculiar in the context) of the word "make-believe,"
with which the "aesthetic attitude" is specifically
identified, and which implies that "aesthetic criticism"
will have nothing to do with any "attitudes to life"
that a book may (incidentally) include—a view directly opposed to that of James himself who has remarked that "the only reason for the existence of a
novel is that it does attempt to represent life." Representation is not make-believe, and a representation of
life in the judgment of which moral evaluations are to
be excluded is one which is at best partial and may be
totally irrelevant. The human judgment must be one
that springs from "our profoundest ethical sensibility,"
because this is at the root of our feeling about what
matters in life and therefore what life is. It has no

necessary connexion with "accepted principles of morality"; and what Leavis says in effect is that James is asking us to accept that certain judgments are right, certain relationships are wholesome, when our conscience tells us that they are not; and that James has not in his work been able to make a revolutionary change—that is, to show us that it is in fact our consciences, our ethical sensibilities, that are shortsighted or misdirected or simply misinformed. What appears to be at fault in Osborne's curious transformation of Leavis' telling phrase into the deadness of his "accepted principles" is partly a simple misunderstanding of the word "our," which must refer to those things basic to our humanity,[13] but which Osborne quite unwarrantably narrows. But beyond this is an assumption—found also, as we have seen in a critic like Ransom whose aesthetics are of Osborne's persuasion—that to speak of the moral content or substance of literature is to refer to a message, a piece of moral wisdom somehow embedded in a literary cake whose main matter is something totally different. The fact is, as Leavis says of one novel in particular, though it is a judgment which bears on them all,

> when we examine the formal perfection of *Emma*, we find that it can be appreciated only in terms of the moral preoccupations that characterize the novelist's peculiar interest in life. Those who suppose it to be an 'aesthetic matter,' a beauty of 'composition' that is combined, miraculously, with 'truth to life,' can give no adequate reason for the view that *Emma* is a great novel, and no intelligent account of its perfection of form.[14]

2

One of the most obvious differences between Leavis' criticism and Winters' is a matter of *tone*. The curious bleakness and remoteness of much of Winters' work, its dead-pan effect on the reader, are largely due to an attitude in the writer which seems to say, "This is how it is—or this is how *I* see it—take it or leave it." But it is plain in all Leavis' work, whether he makes it specific or not, that there is a constant appeal to the reader for agreement—on terms, on criteria, on particular judgments. His conversational mode helps here, of course, for it implies an audience likely (theoretically at least) to become articulate at any time—and more, it implies a two-way process, an exchange. Leavis' well-known formula for critical judgments—"This is so, is it not?"—is an explicit appeal for corroboration put in the form of verbal exchange. As he has said, the question asks for the answer, "Yes, but. . . ." A definitely negative answer would obviously be a surprise, and the formula hardly allows for a divergence so wide as that would imply. To this extent Leavis' characteristic stance may give the appearance of being authoritarian, and Leavis himself something of a bully. I believe this impression is quite wrong; and the question included is seriously meant *as a question*, however much it seems to be tilted in one direction. But what lies behind and gives substance to his use of the formula is a conviction that we do share a fundamental human sensibility which can properly be appealed to in this way. This, as I understand it, is the impersonality referred to by Leavis when he says:

> It is true that our judgments ought to come from an impersonal centre in us, and that we shouldn't have been able to make them but for a truth the statement of which would be a generalized form of Mr. Anderson's proposition: 'If James had not felt in himself the very impulses which he saw crystallized in American manners he would not have understood American manners.' This possibility of impersonality and this measure of 'community of consciousness' are implied in the existence of art.[15]

But if a community of consciousness is implied in the existence of art, so it is in the possibility of criticism. Winters rarely gives any evidence of taking account of it, though something of this nature must be implied by any criticism that aims to be more than merely impressionistic. Thus, while he goes in for much theoretical sharpshooting, Winters' published exchanges with other critics are not in the nature of collaborations. Much of his work, certainly, consists of corrections of theoretical positions assumed by other critics, and restatements of his own in the light of a fresh challenge; but there is a limit to the virtue of repetitions of principle which do not issue in concrete judgments, more particularly in an active exchange aiming to arrive at a placing of the work within a community of values, values which define themselves relatively to one another and to *shared* experience, individually felt but with a more-than-individual resonance, signifying to the individual something of how he stands in relation to the world around him.

Any critic not wholly unaware of the past must be relating his opinions to consensuses of judgments that have been traditionally assented to (and differed from); and any critic not content merely to utter private impressions makes his appeal for agreement of some sort among his readers. But this will hardly amount to collaboration unless the agreement means more than a coincidence of opinion, unless the objective standards which Winters insists on are a function of the very collaboration itself and of the "community of consciousness" which this implies. I have said that most of Leavis' strictures on Johnson can be applied without injustice to Winters. But we can nevertheless see the advantage that Johnson has over the modern instance through being at one with the "common sense" of his time. "Johnson's ear," Leavis has said, "is the product of a training . . . in positive taste, . . . a training in a great positive tradition. . . ." It carried with it, as we should all acknowledge, severe limitations. But all civilizations are limited by their own positive definitions. If the eighteenth century was unduly restricted, our own is not discriminating enough. We have taken away the fetters that shackled Johnson's taste—we have learnt the capacity to enjoy nearly everything—and part of the price is an inability even to understand what is meant by standards. Eighteenth-century habits of mind on the other hand reflected, in part represented, the strength of a decidedly civilized society, and the critic's judgments drew their sanction from the fact that standards were genuinely held in common. Lacking this sanction, Winters' idiosyncrasies come to look like irresponsibility, and even his most acceptable judgments want a certain security of foundation.

My claim, then, prompted by this recall of the character of criticism in a well-defined (if therefore necessarily limited) civilization, is that criticism, in looking for essential agreement, is looking for a human link, and that the standards appealed to are the public face of values inherent in the human fact that no man is an island.

This, as I see it, is what justified the collaborative critical effort of *Scrutiny*; and in such ways *Scrutiny* tended to look upon itself. The very critical process involves an assumption of values that are broadly human and cannot be realized in the isolated individual:

> A judgment is a real judgment, or it is nothing. It must, that is, be a sincere personal judgment; but it aspires to be more than personal. Essentially it has the form: 'This is so, is it not?' But the agreement appealed for must be real, or it serves no critical purpose and can bring no

satisfaction to the critic. What his activity of its very
nature aims at, in fact, is a collaborative exchange or
commerce. Without a many-sided real exchange—the
collaboration by which the object, the poem (for example), in which the individual minds meet, and at the
same time the true judgments concerning it, are
established—the function of criticism cannot be said to
be working. Without a wide coherent public, capable of
making its response felt—capable, that is, of taking a
more or less active part in that collaboration—there is,
for the critic, no effective appeal to standards. For
standards (which are not of the order of the measures in
the Weights and Measures Office) are 'there' only in
and by the collaborative process that criticism essentially
is.[16]

The personal judgment, then, doesn't merely seek
corroboration: it is looking for the common reference
which can only come from a common cause; living is
more than individual, is "collaboration," something
held and done in common, and its inherent values are
not to be found by merely individual effort. Indeed the
kind of standard which this paragraph has in mind
cannot exist for the isolated individual, and cannot be
given any meaning outside of a community of consciousness. So, as an early editorial puts it,

> The critic puts his judgments in the clearest and most
> unevadable form in order to invite response; to forward
> that exchange without which there can be no hope of
> centrality. Centrality is the product of reciprocal pres-
> sures, and a healthy criticism is the play of these.[17]

The reference is again to a "centre"—a word which
must carry echoes of Arnold's "ideal centre of correct
information, taste and intelligence." To Arnold this is
still to some extent exemplified in the world around
him, to be taken in some measure for granted, at least
by an educated mind. He could invite acceptance—at

any rate from those expected to read him—merely by a reference in passing. But for *Scrutiny*, in a state of culture much more fragmentary, it becomes necessary to insist more on what (in practice) a centre implies. For this concept of centrality is itself the centre of a knot of assumptions, beliefs, and attitudes which are frequently referred to and displayed in *Scrutiny*, assumptions in one sense less confident than Arnold's, in so far as they can be taken so little for granted in the larger world as it is. That *Scrutiny* could take them for granted within its own covers is a mark of its strength and its conviction, for it implies a common conception among the contributors of the kind of discipline criticism should be.

Yet it seems to me evident that this conception is not widely understood—one reason, I think, for the hostility and bewilderment that *Scrutiny* gave rise to. Following the passage on collaboration just quoted, Leavis begins a new paragraph: "These elementary truths, surely, are not themselves difficult to grasp." On the contrary, I think that they really are difficult to grasp and that many people, when they have understood what they imply, would not accept them. They imply a special kind of personal integrity and a rejection of a purely individualistic view of our place in society. To revert for a moment to Winters, a main responsibility for the limitations in his critical output must be carried by his refusal or inability to work in concert with those whose basic agreement on function (that is, on values) defines a given sensibility, and at the same time by his inability to draw on the acknowledged common experience of an assured and comprehensive civilization. But of course it is not his fault that he hasn't this coherent civilization at his back. It is one of the great facts of our time that such a civilization exists nowhere—at least outside those countries where totalitarianism may have planted an artificial unanimity: we pay, perhaps, for our freedom and democracy with the loss of a belief in the whole-ness and togetherness of human society, integrated by values which are meaningless to the mere stylite and to the critic addressing himself to stylites. And the experi-ences which this critic will miss are those that only arise in a community recognizing sanctions and re-sponsibilities beyond itself and its individual mem-bers.

The importance of this idea of a community, reiter-ated often enough in *Scrutiny*, is brought to the sur-face in such a statement as this from Leavis' introduc-tion to his anthology of essays from *The Calendar of Modern Letters:*

> Where the recognition of standards of criticism can be counted on, then there is more than the individual; there is also some remnant of tradition, the common mind, the something-more-than-individual that *The Calendar* refers to in its "Valediction":
>
>> The value of a review must be judged by its attitude to the living literature of the time (which includes such works of the past as can be absorbed by the con-temporary sensibility). . . .
>
> When there is a "living literature of the time" there is also a "contemporary sensibility," and it is always the business of criticism (whatever it may appear to be doing immediately) to define—that is, help to form—and organize this, and to make conscious the "standards" implicit in it.[18]

The public to which the critic can appeal, in which standards are maintained, is one "embodying a certain collective experience, intelligence and taste."

And it is through this contemporary sensibility that what energy there is in the literary world becomes more generally available. It is through a public defined in this way, and

> through the conditions of general education implied in the existence of such a public, that literature, as the critic is concerned with it, can reasonably be thought of as influencing contemporary affairs and telling in realms in which literary critics are not commonly supposed to count for much.[19]

I should not want to suggest that all those who wrote for *Scrutiny* would necessarily accept this account and these deductions from their practice. The word "community" itself might seem ill-chosen, and "culture" might be preferred. Johnson, we read

> could rejoice to concur with the 'common reader' because taste was then in the keeping of the educated who, sharing a homogeneous culture, maintained in tradition a surer taste than any that is merely individual can be, and he could not have imagined such an authority being seriously challenged.[20]

But "culture" is a difficult word, which has undergone a fair battering in recent years, and means many things to many people. Lionel Trilling, for example, who seemed at one time much bothered by it, defined culture on one occasion as "the locus of the meeting of literature with social actions and attitudes." [21] This, though a little too consciously modern in its phrasing, might really have something to do with, say, Augustan culture; but it is surely much too specialized, and it does little to indicate what it might be to *live* in a homogeneous culture, one which took certain great values in life as not seriously to be challenged. Elsewhere Trilling has described culture in terms which seem to rule out any kind of cumulative acceptance or understanding:

A culture is not a flow, nor even a confluence; the form of its existence is struggle, or at least debate—it is nothing if not a dialectic. And in any culture there are likely to be certain artists who contain a large part of the dialectic within themselves, their meaning and power lying in their contradictions; they contain within themselves, it may be said, the very essence of the culture, and the sign of this is that they do not submit to serve the ends of any one ideological group or tendency.[22]

The main weakness here, as Trilling tries earnestly to say what culture is like, is that he gives no clue to the way in which any particular culture may be defined. Even if all cultures are debates, not all debates are cultures; and the contradictions are not the most important things to emphasize. Trilling is a little nearer in saying that by "culture" "we must mean not merely the general social condition . . . but also a particular congeries of formulated ideas." [23]

Now undoubtedly these are important aspects of a culture: if we go back to the early eighteenth century we can certainly see that formulated ideas are prominent and important. But they need not always be; and in what we should call "folk-cultures" they play hardly any part. Moreover, all Trilling's attempts to point to the nature of a culture leave out something which Leavis has obviously considered essential. For the taste that was "surer . . . than any that is merely individual" was maintained in *tradition*, a word much used in *Scrutiny* to indicate (with "community") our own link with the past and the present of our race. The culture which *Scrutiny* was concerned for was "a spiritual force that can direct and determine" and was intimately linked with tradition:

It is to the culture that transcends the individual as the language he inherits transcends him that we come back; to the culture that has decayed with tradition. The

standards maintained in such a tradition, . . . constitute a surer taste than any individual can pretend to.
And it is not merely a matter of literary taste. The
culture in question, which is not, indeed, identical with
literary tradition but which will hardly survive it, is a
sense of relative value and a memory—such wisdom as
constitutes the residuum of the general experience. It
lives only in individuals, but individuals can live without
it; and where they are without it they do not know what
they miss. And the world, troubled as it is, is unaware of
what is gone.[24]

It would perhaps be stretching a point to claim that
the sanctions invoked here are explicitly religious,
though the reference, as other excerpts will make clear,
is certainly to a culture which has more than a casual
link with traditional pieties. Tradition, both within
and without literature, is more than a solemn way of
speaking of succession. For it stresses continuity and
the possibilities of inherited wisdom. Leavis, it is well-
known, sees the literary tradition as now having to bear
the whole task of keeping alive the continuity of
consciousness, the "conservation of the collective experience." This opens very large questions which I cannot go into here, though it may be worth remarking
that if this task is now all to be borne by the literary
tradition, then the relations between literature and
criticism, on the one hand, and the culture of a whole
people on the other, will be something different from
what they have ever been before. I do not mean to
suggest that there has been no relation between them
when a continuity that was much more than a literary
one might be found. There is every reason to accept
the argument that the writings of, say, Shakespeare
and Bunyan, grew from much more than a literary
tradition. But folk-cultures have got along very well
without literature, and most cultures of any sort often

pay literature scant attention. Leavis acknowledges that a concentration entirely on literature as the prop of tradition implies using it as a substitute:

> What we have lost is the organic community with the living culture it embodied. Folk-songs, folk-dances, Cotswold cottages and handicraft products are signs and expressions of something more: an art of life, a way of living, ordered and patterned, involving social arts, codes of intercourse and a responsive adjustment, growing out of immemorial experience, to the natural environment and the rhythm of the year.[25]

It seems to be common form now to doubt whether the organic community ever existed; and no doubt a good deal more than an art of living, etc., was often involved. Raymond Williams is a fair example of this skepticism, remarking that "if there is one thing certain about 'the organic community,' it is that it has always gone."[26] I think that the illustrations that Leavis gives are enough to prove that a closely-knit, rhythmic life did exist in English villages in the past, though I am less than certain that it is *altogether* of the past. It is perhaps more to the point in the present discussion to realize how *un*literary such a culture must have been (and still is insofar as it survives). For it could only stay alive by remaining below the level of consciousness, whereas a literary tradition would seem to demand the reverse. The addition of a literary element to a culture of this kind would mark its decay as surely as anything.[27]

The student of Leavis' literary criticism (conscious of the rather different use made of "tradition" in *Revaluation* and in the book which works the word significantly into its title) may perhaps play down the importance to him of the concept introduced in this fragment. But "community" is nonetheless a word of which he ought to take serious note. For here the religious implications are more in evidence, and more definite: "the rhythm of the year" is not invoked casually. And it seems to me that it reflects an attitude necessarily implied in speaking of a "sense of relative value" to be preserved in the "memory" of the race, an attitude which gains its sanction from ways of living which cannot be described other than in religious terms.

Now I think it is noticeable that Leavis' whole attitude becomes more explicitly religious, more concerned to evoke religious explanations, in his later work, no doubt partly through the experience of his study of Lawrence. But there is no break in continuity; the comparatively early chapter on Wordsworth in *Revaluation* shows Leavis already willing to use the word "religious" to describe the particular value of Wordsworth's poetry—not only what Wordsworth himself invoked, but its peculiar value for us today. And it seems natural to suppose that, when Leavis writes that "it is not wisdom that stops at advocating the free play of individual sensibility. Indeed, the truly living sensibility cannot be content to be merely individual and merely free," [28] he has in mind that exclamation of Lawrence's which he is so fond of quoting, "Thank God I am not free, any more than a rooted tree is free."

By way of producing an additional reference in a wide field, I should like to call attention to the very interesting analysis of the tradition of European culture to be found in Sir Max Beloff's book *Europe and the Europeans*. For my purpose, the most relevant section of this chapter contains an illustration of the continuity of the European artistic tradition in the light of three characteristic paintings produced in Northern Europe between 1450 and 1650. I quote his description of Van Eyck's *Betrothal of Arnolfini:*

It would be impossible to describe, let alone interpret, the inwardness of this painting without reference to fourteen hundred years of traditional pieties. How else could we explain the thoughtful and dignified expression of the two figures, each of whom is clearly impressed by the sacredness of the occasion? The very purpose of the picture must have evoked in them, and in the painter, a sense of solemnity, for this is not only a picture but a document: the painter has actually put his name centrally on the wall behind, over the little round mirror which reflects his presence at the ceremony to which he attests: *Johannes de Eyck fuit hic*. The man has assumed a specially earnest posture, with his pale lean hand raised in an oath of fealty. To be sure, this is not a Southern interpretation: there are here no angels, no *putti*, no clouds, no attendant saints, no priest, no crucifix. There is no least suggestion of nature in deliquescence. Yet, for all its realism—the shoes on the floor, the beads on the wall, the effect of light on the garments, the careful painting of the dog, the sturdy Northern refusal to soften or abrade any least item of actuality according to the current Platonic concepts of ideal beauty in the South, this is a deeply religious picture. If we wished, incidentally, to give our Oriental an illustration of European culture (or of any culture) not as dispensable decoration added to life but as something that is part and parcel of it, here is the perfect example.[29]

So much, one may say, for "significant form." Beloff has not only given a convincing description of the picture: he has said enough to show that "part and parcel" is too weak a phrase—culture is here the very framework of life, a whole habit of living—and he has also shown that this is the only kind of description that would be at all adequate. It is, incidentally, an excellent example of how impossible it is to talk in terms of pure art when faced with a work with any human reference.

Beloff's perception is guided and conditioned by his power of discrimination, which is itself a moral power, a power of human judgment. And for all the objectivity of his description and its sticking closely to what is there on canvas in front of him, he cannot avoid conveying (I don't mean that he has tried to) the esteem in which he holds the picture, even though his appreciation does not necessarily involve him in sharing its pieties. But "piety" implies a reference to something transcending the individual, and Beloff is certainly right that the posture and expressions of the two figures are really unintelligible without an understanding of the religious significance of the occasion. Needless to say, this does not imply that the religious colouring, the religious attitude to the occasion are necessarily justified or proper. But to implicate in one's criticism the residual general experience of the race is to make use of a tradition inseparable from a religious commitment which has linked very different communities at very different times. The insistence on the need to conserve "the collective experience" is an appeal essentially pious in all that it implies.

In Leavis' chapter on Wordsworth we find these implications made explicit—though not more so than the nature of the criticism demands: it is always Wordsworth who is at the centre of the critic's interest, not some abstract theory or equivalence. Notably, however, Leavis, who is concerned for the value of Wordsworth's work *to the present-day sensibility*, draws upon those aspects of the poetry which link Wordsworth most clearly to the general human condition. Wordsworth's poetry, he suggests, was the answer (for Wordsworth) to the question; "How, in a world which has shown itself to be like this, is it possible to go on living?" The answer, to be valid or even relevant for more than Wordsworth alone, must be in terms which involve his personal problems and needs in the wider issues of humanity.

> For if his problem was personal, it was not selfishly so, not merely self-regarding; and it is also a general one: if (and how shall he not?) the sensitive and imaginative freely let their 'hearts lie open' to the suffering of the world, how are they to retain any health or faith for living? . . . [Wordsworth's] sense of responsibility for human distress and his generously active sympathies had involved him in emotional disasters that threatened his hold on life. A disciplined limiting of contemplation to the endurable, and, consequently, a withdrawal to a reassuring environment, became terrible necessities for him.[30]

The withdrawal Leavis sees not as an escape from the world, but as an inherently human self-discipline; as he says, Wordsworth cannot be accused of weakness or cowardice. Wordsworth

> stands for a distinctly human naturalness; one, that is, consummating a discipline, moral and other. A poet who can bring home to us the possibility of such a naturalness should to-day be found important. In Wordsworth's poetry the possibility is offered us realized—realized in a mode central and compelling enough to enforce the bearing of poetry upon life, the significance of this poetry for actual living. The absence both of the specifically sexual in any recognizable form and of any sign of repression serves to emphasize this significance, the significance of this achieved natural-ness, spontaneous, and yet the expression of an order and the product of an emotional and moral training. . . . Wordsworth was, on the showing of his poetry and everything else, normally and robustly hu-man. The selectiveness and the habit of decorum in-volved in 'recollection in tranquility' were normal and, in a wholly laudatory sense of the word, conventional; that is, so endorsed by common usage as to be natural.[31]

The stress here lies both on the discipline and on its naturalness; it is not possible to separate the two. The value of the discipline—its value for Wordsworth, and its value for his readers—lies essentially in its being common, in its human naturalness. But this naturalness is itself "the expression of an order," which means more than something merely self-imposed. It is linked closely with the very withdrawal which to many has signified Wordsworth's loss of interest in humanity. And Leavis, in justifying and assessing the present importance of the poetry, its significance for actual living, must relate it in terms which link the patterns of individual human lives with "something that transcends" them.

> Wordsworth's preoccupation was with a distinctly human naturalness, with sanity and spiritual health, and his interest in mountains was subsidiary. His mode of preoccupation, it is true, was that of a mind intent always upon ultimate sanctions, and upon the living connexions between man and the extra-human universe; it was, that is, in the same sense as Lawrence's was, religious.[32]

I think that the force of Leavis' criticism is to suggest that this "mode of preoccupation," which was so very necessary to Wordsworth, is an essential defining condition of the discipline, and is intimately linked with its naturalness (a habit "so endorsed by common usage as to be natural").

Writing of James in *The Great Tradition*, Leavis has said that he

> had no such immediate sense of human solidarity, no such nourishing intuition of the unity of life, as could make up to him for the deficiencies of civilized intercourse: life for him must be humane or it was nothing. There was nowhere in his work that preoccupation with ultimate sanctions which we may call religious.[33]

Leavis here almost identifies "that preoccupation with ultimate sanctions" with the "nourishing intuition of the unity of life": this sense of the peculiarly religious nature of a full involvement in life is clearly of a piece with his intimate understanding of Lawrence (who is invoked, in fact, in the sentence immediately before those just quoted). In his book on Lawrence, there is naturally much emphasis on the religious quality of a full human relationship—most emphatically in the chapter on *The Rainbow*, which is significantly called 'Lawrence and Tradition' and has much to say on the pieties and conventions of the traditional way of life against which the personal dramas are played out. The effect of the whole long chapter is to lay peculiar emphasis on the "transcendent" nature of the needs of Lawrence's (and by implication all) people. But the most explicit invocation of religious sanctions comes in a comment on a passage describing Tom Brangwen's direct submission to the external order of the universe. Here is the passage in Lawrence:

> But during the long February nights with the ewes in labour, looking out from the shelter into the flashing stars, he knew he did not belong to himself. He must admit that he was only fragmentary, something incomplete and subject. There were the stars in the dark heaven travelling, the whole host passing by on some eternal voyage. So he sat small and submissive to the greater ordering.[34]

Leavis' comment, drawing on the particular human drift of the whole book, culminates in this profound and revealing sentence:

> What, in fact, strikes us as religious is the intensity with his men and women, hearkening to their deepest needs and promptings as they seek 'fulfilment' in marriage, know that they 'do not belong to themselves,' but are responsible to something that, in transcending the individual, transcends love and sex too.[35]

But there is one essay in which Leavis foreshadows the conclusions of his book on Lawrence, an essay with a curiously personal flavour—curiously, because its subject, which is tragedy, amounts for Leavis to a discovery of a kind of experience which is impersonal:

> it is an essential part of the definition of the tragic that it breaks down, or undermines and supersedes, such attitudes [which insist on the privacy and absolute independence of each personality]. It establishes below them a kind of profound impersonality in which experience matters, not because it is mine—because it is to me it belongs or happens, or because it subserves or issues in purpose or will, but because it is what it is, the 'mine' mattering only in so far as the individual sentience is the indispensable focus of experience.[36]

In using the word "personal," I mean—what is very clear within the context of this passage—that such statements have the poignancy of a discovery personally made, and one whose effect on the individual is movingly present to us. It is, moreover, the discovery of a positive value unlike those that are an enriching of a merely individual life:

> the experience is constructive or creative, and involves a recognizing positive value as in some way defined and vindicated by death. It is as if we were challenged at the profoundest level with the question, 'In what does the significance of life reside?', and found ourselves contemplating, for answer, a view of life, and of the things, giving it value, that makes the valued appear unquestionably more important than the valuer, so that significance lies, clearly and inescapably, in the willing adhesion of the individual self to something other than itself.[37]

This plainly is the statement of a religious conviction: and here the adherence to the "something other," the recognition of "something" that transcends the individual is the acceptance of the "link" at a deeper level than that of personality. I should add that I am not sure of the status of one term in this argument. In the first passage quoted, there seems to be a separation of the experience from the person who experiences. I do not really understand how an experience can be defined apart from the person who owns it and am not even sure it can be *conceived* apart—which is perhaps what Leavis means by the qualification at the end of this paragraph. But experience is not something having a shadowy existence in the void, which then finds itself through such an individual focus: it only exists in terms of the individual who has it, though experiences which seem to go unusually deep do often have the temporary effect on the individual of an emptying out of all personality. In the second paragraph quoted, experience and the individual sentience give way to the valued and the valuer. And here the terms raise no such problem; for the valued, though living in intimate relation to the individual, can be conceived—can have its existence—apart from any particular sentience.

The religious judgment here is not something distinct from the literary one—it is not the "completion" that Eliot asked for: there is only one judgment, yet it is the outcome of an experience attained through poetry. It thus takes its terms from the poetic experience, going no further into particular definition than the poetry allows. So far as I know, Leavis has never in his published writing been more precise about the "something that transcends." And as literary critic he need not be: indeed it would be inappropriate to go further than is necessary to make clear his grounds for using the word "religious" and any special emphasis he needs to lay. These grounds are, I think, explicit enough in such of Leavis' more general statements as I have quoted, and a more precise focus comes in the individual judgments. A more limiting statement of a specific religious viewpoint is irrelevant to the literary criticism which asks for a free play of the intelligence on literature; "completion" by criticism from "a definite theological standpoint" is (as, indeed, Eliot insists) not literary criticism, and it will, one may feel, encourage sectarian distortions. It is in fact a mark of the tact and sense of relevance of Leavis' literary criticism that, in spite of his refusing to stop short of invoking religious sanctions, one cannot tell from his criticism what more specific religious position he holds.

Leavis has, it seems to me, developed his critical position to the point where religious references are more or less bound to become explicit. He is not alone, even among critics who see the need to maintain the strict relevance of literary criticism. Winters himself has made this rather solemn confession:

> I am aware that my absolutism implies a theistic position, unfortunate as this admission may be. If experience appears to indicate that absolute truths exist, that we are able to work toward an approximate apprehension of them, but that they are antecedent to our apprehension and that our apprehension is seldom and perhaps never perfect, then there is only one place in which those truths may be located, and I see no way to escape this conclusion.[38]

If Winters really feels that the admission is unfortunate, then a slightly less naïve philosophy might save him the bother. It seems unreasonable to balance a belief in God on such a precarious version of Platonic realism.[39]

But the real nuisance of this account, I suggest, is not to God, but to ourselves, insofar as it makes the truths so immobile and unyielding. If Winters' observation of literature and life has led him to see shadowy absolute truths here and there among the trees, we receive no impression that these truths are the meeting-place of different human experiences seeking common and inclusive statement. Yet this is, if he wants it, the foundation of a critic's "natural religion."

Leavis' position, for all the delicacy with which it is expressed, implies a more whole-hearted acceptance: it has much more of the dignity of personal conviction through experience. Returning to the book on Lawrence, we find a passage which gives us, as Buckley says, the whole matter in miniature.

> Lawrence is the greatest kind of creative writer; it can be said of him, as of Flaubert or T. S. Eliot it cannot, that his radical attitude towards life is positive; looking for a term with which to indicate its nature, we have to use 'reverence.' But 'reverence' must not be allowed to suggest any idealizing bent; and if we say that the reverence expresses itself in a certain essential tenderness, we don't mean that Lawrence is 'tender-minded' or in the least sentimentally given. The attitude is one of strength, and it is clairvoyant and incorruptible in its preoccupation with realities. It expresses, of course, the rare personal adequacy of an individual of genius, but it is also the product of a fine and mature civilization, the sanctions, the valuations, and the pieties of which speak through the individual.[40]

Lawrence called himself a passionately religious man; and Leavis has claimed that it is he (Lawrence), and not the "officially Christian" Eliot and Mauriac and Waugh, who has a truly religious sense of human dignity. In this passage we find the characteristic *timbre* of Lawrence's preoccupation with reality identified; and, significantly, related to the soil from which he grew. The total attitude is "one of strength" . . . "the product of a fine and mature civilization, the sanctions, the valuations, and the pieties of which speak through the individual." [41]

"Centrality . . . the product of reciprocal pressures." I am suggesting that this conception of centrality implies a belief in the possibility of the kind of civilization that Leavis invokes in giving us Lawrence's background, or of something that, without too much loss, can take its place.[42] It implies that standards are not created individually; but initial individual judgments are confirmed, amended, chastened, and amplified in an experience of living which is more than any individual can contain and where personal needs and achievements meet in the creation of the standards by which a civilization lives. For the whole idea of a standard implies a reference which is beyond any individual but contains them all. There is no such thing as a "pure" experience any more than there can be a completely free individual:

> One cannot suppose it either possible or desirable to go on 'experiencing' as if there had been nothing before. And with the beginnings of maturity the problem of organization becomes one for serious effort; taken seriously, it leads to a discipline and a training, emotional and intellectual, designed to 'preserve the individual from the solely centrifugal impulse of heresy, to make him capable of judging for himself, and at the same time capable of judging and understanding the judgments of the experience of the race.' [43]

The linking of the individual judgment with an experience that transcends that of any individual but is yet achieved only through the individual experience, is the foundation of any possible centrality, any possible community, any possible religion. And in these terms the function of art implies a gathering together, less the communicating and preserving of local experience than the realization through the individual of the finest and most profound potentialities of the race.

BURKE'S METHOD IN ACTION

A MAIN DEFECT in Burke's critical method is that he is apt to train his sights before the object to be aimed at comes into view. It would not be quite fair to say that the object has *no* effect on the direction chosen; but often an aspect is selected which is partial and may lead to serious distortions and misreadings. The essay 'Symbolic Action in a Poem by Keats' [1] *starts* with the assumption that the famous aphorism at the end of the *Ode on a Grecian Urn* is an assertion of the identity of poetry and science, the "aesthetic" and the "practical" ("'truth' being the essential word of knowledge [science] and 'beauty' being the essential word of art or poetry").[2] What happens after this is summarized in Burke's own words at the end of the essay:

> The poem begins with an ambiguous fever which in the course of the further development is "separated out," splitting into a bodily fever and a spiritual counterpart. The bodily passion is the malign aspect of the fever, the mental action its benign aspect. In the course of the development, the malign passion is transcended and the benign active partner, the intellectual exhilaration, takes over. At the beginning, where the two aspects were ambiguously one, the bodily passion would be the "scene" of the mental action. . . . But as the two become separated out, the mental action transcends the

bodily passion. It becomes an act in its own right, making discoveries and assertions not grounded in the bodily passion. And this quality of action, in transcending the merely physical symptoms of the fever, would thus require a different ground or scene, one more suited in quality to the quality of the transcendent act.

The transcendent act is concretized, or "materialized" in the vision of the "immortal" scene, the reference in Stanza IV to the original scene of the Urn, the "heavenly" scene of a dead, or immortal, Greece (the scene in which the Urn was originally enacted and which is also fixed on its face). . . .

This transcendent scene is the level at which the earthly laws of contradiction no longer prevail. Hence, in the terms of this scene, he can proclaim the unity of truth and beauty (of science and art), a proclamation which he needs to make precisely because here was the basic split responsible for the romantic agitation (in both poetic and philosophic idealism). That is, it was gratifying to have the oracle proclaim the unity of poetry and science because the values of technology and business were causing them to be at odds. And from the perspective of a "higher level" (the perspective of a dead or immortal scene transcending the world of temporal contradictions) the split could be proclaimed once more a unity.

At this point, at this stage of exaltation, the fever has been replaced by chill. But the bodily passion has completely dropped out of account. All is now mental action. Hence, the chill (as in the ecstatic exclamation, "Cold Pastoral!") is proclaimed only in its benign aspect.[3]

As the summary indicates, a good many things extrinsic to what the poem actually says are brought into the account. There is the (almost inevitable) political reference, there are the generalizings about romanticism, and, most important, there are the promptings given by the introduction of well-known material about Keats's illness when the poem was written. It seems that Burke felt some uneasiness about making use of information of this kind: "I grant that such speculations interfere with the symmetry of criticism as a game." [4] Criticism has more important things to do than play games of symmetry; and one may well seek abroad for all the help one can get—the test should be one of relevance to the poem. Burke, however, slips with alarming ease from the fact that the poem was written during a particular illness to the assumption that the illness is actually the *subject* of the poem—another instance, perhaps, of the genetic fallacy. The fever that he refers to is, in its physical, "malign" aspect, the tuberculosis from which Keats died; and the poem is a progressive separating out of the benign, "transcendent" aspect of this same fever until "the bodily passion has completely dropped out of account." Burke therefore *links* the "breathing human passion" of Stanza III with the frozen (non-human) love depicted on the urn, whereas the definite tendency, of this stanza at least, seems to be to oppose them. Burke explains his view thus:

> There is a transcendental fever, which is felicitous, divinely above "all breathing human passion." And this "leaves" the other level, the level of earthly fever, "a burning forehead and a parching tongue." From the bodily fever, which is a passion, and malign, there has split off a spiritual activity, a wholly benign aspect of the total agitation.[5]

This interpretation, which is the lynchpin of Burke's account, depends on taking "that" in line 9 of Stanza III to qualify "happy love" in line 5. Unfortunately the punctuation, syntax, and all other evidence point to its qualifying "passion" in line 8. And the correct reading is surely that the happy love is far above the breathing human passion, the effect of which (the breathing passion) is to leave with us a heart high-sorrowful and so forth. The "love" on the urn is superior in that, never having "breathed," it can never change or turn to anguish. And I cannot think that it is right to suggest, as Burke does, that it is the love on the urn—and not the bodily passion—which is essentially active (Burke makes too much too cleverly of the root meaning of "passion"): the poem seems to me to insist on the stillness, the fact that all movement on the urn is unchangeably frozen. It is fair to say, however, that Keats somewhat confuses things by describing the happy love as forever *panting,* which does indeed sound like an active kind of breathing.[6] Yet the active tendency of the word is contradicted by "forever"; the melodist is unwearied because he *cannot* be tired, and the mad pursuit and struggle to escape of the opening are made only when the human interpretation of the unmoving picture is imposed upon them.

Burke traces the "definitive" separation between the benign and malign aspects of the fever which he finds in Stanza III back to a mere possibility of "two levels of motivation" in Stanza I. It has never been altogether clear to me what Burke really means by "motive" and "motivation." In the present instance there is a kind of gloss a little later, when he speaks of "the two motives, the action and the passion."[7] And the fever must therefore be ambiguous because we don't know in Stanza I which of these two "motives" characterizes what is being described. (Lines 5–8 "express a doubt whether the figures on the urn are 'deities or mortals'—and the motives of gods are of a different order from the motives of men."[8]) But it is not true that the poem begins with an ambiguous fever. It begins with an address to the urn and a series of self-questionings about what the pictures on it represent.

And it is essential to the mood and the attitude of the poem that these remain pictures and therefore *static*. (The urn will remain unmoved, unchanging, in later times, in midst of other woe; and this is its special virtue for Keats, just as the love scene depicted is superior as being frozen in the moment before ecstasy turns to pain and disillusionment.)

If one doesn't mind the irrelevance of its opening and ignores the faulty reading of Stanza III, one may say that Burke's essay is a fairly entertaining fantasy on ideas suggested by looking into Keats's *Grecian Urn*. But as Burke claims to be producing a piece of criticism, the poem itself naturally (and properly) keeps popping up; and at each return—particularly near the end—the lack of connectedness is patent and shows Burke to be remarkably insensitive to tone. Most readers have, I think, felt that Stanza IV has more than a hint of the shrewder Keats who cannot remain in his ecstatic opposition of the urn's wonderful suspension to the ordinary business of living. These readers give full force to "emptied" and "silent" and "desolate"—words implying that all is *not* perfect in the vision on the urn. This stanza has a weaker effect than the corresponding sections of the *Nightingale* ode, where Keats vividly demonstrates the impossibility of escaping from "the weariness, the fever and the fret" in a vision which does not last. The desolate town may now be responsible for the cold of the last stanza; and certainly the scene in Stanza IV is not "transcendent": the attentive reader is not likely to find its imagery "that of communication with the immortal or the dead" [9]—except so far as all the scenes on the urn represent *some* communication with a vanished past—unless he has been predisposed by special personal inclination to find it so.

Nevertheless Keats obviously has little trouble in

returning, in his last five lines, to the mood of ecstatic contemplation of aesthetic stillness which has been uppermost through the earlier stanzas. In such a frame of mind it then becomes natural to take the famous aphorism as asserting not the identity of poetry and science or "act" and "scene" but an attitude to living in which the highest perfection is found in some kind of aesthetic contemplation explicitly severed from everyday activity and all breathing *human* passions.

I find the logic of Burke's account of the close of the poem (so far as I can understand it) spurious. He is always up to entering a "thus" or an "and so" at needed moments; but the cogency of the connectives is often illusory:

> This transcendent scene [in Stanza IV] is the level at which the earthly laws of contradiction no longer prevail. Hence, in the terms of this scene, he can proclaim the unity of truth and beauty (of science and art).[10]

From the "perspective of a higher level . . . transcending the world of temporal contradictions" one could presumably proclaim almost anything. The point is not only that this would scarcely bring much consolation to later generations (and so make the urn a friend to man), but that it is quite arbitrary as a conclusion to Burke's previous "demonstration." Furthermore it is not what Keats said.

WINTERS AND ELIOT

VINCENT BUCKLEY reproves Winters for his error in assuming that Eliot (in calling poetry "autotelic") removed poetry completely from life. Buckley goes on:

> He [Winters] notes that, in 'The Function of Criticism,' Eliot holds poetry to be 'autotelic,' and he comments: 'Art, then, is about itself.' The comment is the result of a wrong-headed refusal to see the vagueness of the word 'about,' which Winters uses but Eliot does not. The weakness of Eliot's statement on the self-consistency of art lies elsewhere—in its failure to do more than state that a relationship exists, or to indicate its nature and dynamism.[1]

As a matter of fact Eliot does use the word "about" in such a way ("criticism is . . . *about* something other than itself")[2] as to imply enough essential distinction to justify Winters' rejoinder. And the real weakness in Eliot's statement seems to me to be more that he simply hadn't thought out what he said, and the result was confusion.

Nor does Buckley's explanation of another passage from "The Function of Criticism" help to clear up its deficiencies:

> He [Eliot] does not deny to the *artist* awareness of his function—his function is, seemingly, to bring his re-

sources of feeling, thought, and language to bear on his subject in such a way as to produce a self-contained reality. He is concerned with the *reality* of his poem, and his function is to ensure it. But it is not his job to know what is the *end* of his activity, the function of his own concern with function, or what use is to be made of it by others, or at what point it is to enter and affect the body of society. Poetry is important enough to be treated in its own terms, as a separate thing. Therefore Eliot refuses for the time being to speculate on the results which poetry may have in society in general or in human affairs at all.[3]

I don't believe that Buckley knows what he is talking about: his esoteric distinction between "function" and the "function of a concern with function" is mere verbiage. Nor can the function of bringing the poet's resources ("of feeling, thought, and language" — what a loose lot) to bear, be discussed without this apparently second-order function. Eliot's refusal to speculate on the effects of poetry is a refusal to speculate on poetry, for it is essentially *not* a "separate thing" or a "self-contained reality." This stress on the "reality" of a poem as opposed to its relevance, its live interest for us, only confirms one's suspicions that neither Eliot nor Buckley sorted out his ideas of what poetry is. A self-contained reality does not bring a guarantee of its own importance.

Winters' criticism of Eliot's views on thought and emotion in poetry and of the doctrine of the objective correlative seem extremely shrewd and thoroughly justified. On another issue, however, Winters, I think, comes off less impressively. This is the question of "dramatic immediacy," which he introduces with the help of a quotation from F. O. Matthiessen, who writes, "the dramatic element in poetry lies simply in its power to communicate a sense of real life, a sense of *the immediate present*—that is, of the full quality of a moment as it is actually felt to consist." Winters comments:

> What Eliot means by the dramatic in lyrical poetry, one can only deduce as best one is able: the combination of Homer and the minor writers of the Greek anthology, for example, gives one ample opportunity to think at large. The notion, derived by most of his disciples, however, and one of the two upon which they most commonly act, is indicated by the phrase *the immediate present*, which is italicized in Matthiessen's commentary. Poetry is dramatic—and hence good—in so far as it produces the illusion that the experience described is taking place in the immediate present.[4]

Eliot is surely not the centre of Winters' interest here; but is his gloss even an accurate statement of what Matthiessen says? What evidence is there that Matthiessen intends that the immediate present should be put across as an *illusion?* Matthiessen seems concerned less with the presentness of the moment than with its "full quality." If the moment of experience itself has value, then it is presumably a good thing for it to be given with as much of its quality as possible. And the dramatic technique of, say, *Spelt from Sibyl's Leaves,* in which the working out of the parable is seen within the poem itself, gives an instance of the power (though also, perhaps, of the melodrama) that can result. But for Winters this is an illusion, a deception practised by the poet on his readers. The poem is essentially a meditation on the experience, so that any attempt to present the experience itself in its greatest possible directness is a sham:

> what, after all, is a poem, if we approach it in my own innocent state of mind? It is a statement about an experience, real or imagined. The statement must follow

the experience in time: Donne, for example, could not have written *The Ecstasy* while engaged in the experience described. The poem is a commentary upon something that has happened; it is an act of meditation. The poem is more valuable than the event by virtue of its being an act of meditation: it is the event plus the understanding of the event. Why then should the poet be required to produce the illusion of the immediate experience without intervention of the understanding? Perhaps the understanding is supposed to occur surreptitiously, while the poet is pretending that something else is occurring. But what is the value of such deception? Is it assumed that understanding itself is not a "real" form of experience? The practical effect of the doctrine of dramatic immediacy is to encourage a more or less melodramatic emotionalism.[5]

Now Winters himself argues that what one responds to in a poem is the poet's judgment of his experience; but to be able ourselves to see the judgment for what it is, we must see the experience for what it is. It is when the experience as presented in the poem is inadequate to the emotion attached to it that we should call the poem over-emotional or sentimental (which is exactly what Winters has said of Hopkins and for just the same reasons: the fearful emotion in *No worst, there is none* is not justified by a presented experience). To account for this, Winters' phrase, "the event plus the understanding of the event," is quite inadequate. The need is that the experience should come alive for the reader, and this may or may not involve a "dramatic" presentment (Donne used the method quite frequently, for example, in *The Good Morrow* or in a different way in the *Nocturnal*). Consider Yeats's *The Fascination of What's Difficult,* not a very important poem nor one containing any great dramatic gesture towards its meaning: nonetheless the heavy dragging rhythm gives a feel of the poet's experience so that one is able to judge the implied "commentary" for what it is worth and can see that the experience is not faked. The same may be said of all successful poems. They have the quality that the experience shown is real within the poem—it is something that has really happened and is seen as giving rise to the emotion with which it is contemplated. This seems to be what Matthiessen was saying—or at least what he should have been saying—in talking of the "full quality of the moment." There is no deception implied, no surreptitiousness: of course understanding is a real form of experience, but Winters must surely see that the experience he talks about (here he refers to it as the event) is different from the experience of understanding it, in that the understanding is a second-order experience dependent on the initial one. There must first be something to be understood; and it is the relation between the two experiences that matters. Thus it is that one must have a chance of getting to grips with what the poet says he is feeling emotions about—a chance that Bridges in the poem Winters is so fond of doesn't give us.

On Eliot's determinism and his dogma of "impersonality" Winters does some crisp and efficient demolition. Eliot was very often a slipshod thinker, though not always quite as stupid as Winters makes him out. Nor do I think that Winters' own implied views about the relation of the poet to his own time are very satisfactory. Answering Eliot's jeer at those who hold that poetry shall be "representative of its age," Winters writes:

> But it is primarily Eliot and a small handful of his influential disciples, not the rest of us, who demand that our poetry shall be representative of its age; and they appear to have decided consciously that the unconscious tendency of the age is to produce poetry in the manner

of Pound and Eliot, except when one of them by some unaccountable atavism occasionally happens to feel a liking for a poet of some other kind.[6]

Winters on the other hand holds that

A poet is conditioned by his time to this extent, that it offers him most of his subject-matter; but what he does with that subject-matter—led me insist at the risk of excommunication—is very largely the result of his own intelligence and talent.[7]

Who would disagree, beyond countering the slight tendency of this statement towards a romantic account of inspiration? Eliot hardly would have, and he might have been surprised to find that it was one of his "central ideas" that "art is deteriorating, but it must deteriorate to express honestly the general deterioration of man." I take it that Eliot saw the poet as a focus in which the best thought and feeling of his age is brought as near perfection as possible. The *great* poet writes his time in that he is its most distinguished representative: far as Dante and Shakespeare may have transcended their times, they also very much belonged to them, depending greatly on traditions inherent in them. The subject-matter, the current of thought of the time, enriching as it must have been for the greatness of such poets to have come to such fruition, must to a greater or less extent have conditioned what could be done with it. As for the unconscious tendency of the age being thought by Eliot (and his "disciples") to write in the manner of Pound and Eliot, the question is not whether there is a *tendency* this way or that, but what kind of technique is adequate to the significant experience of a poet alive in his own time. (The poet who is not alive in and to his own time will not be alive for posterity.) Winters has no doubts about this matter:

There is current at present a very general opinion that it is impossible in our time to write good poetry in the mode, let us say, of Bridges, either because of the kind of poetry that has been written since ("the stylistic advances of Eliot and of Pound"), or because of social conditions ("the chaos of modern thought"), or because of both, or because of something else. I believe this to be a form of group hypochondria. The simple fact of the matter is, that it is harder to imitate Bridges than to imitate Pound or Eliot, as it is harder to appreciate him, because Bridges is a finer poet and a saner man; he knows more than they, and to meet him on his own ground we must know more than to meet them.[8]

Eliot's answer to this would have been, I take it, in the terms used in his famous essay on Johnson:

Sensibility alters from generation to generation in everybody, whether we will or no; but expression is only altered by a man of genius. A great many second-rate poets, in fact, are second-rate just for this reason, that they have not the sensitiveness and consciousness to perceive that they feel differently from the preceding generation, and therefore must use words differently.[9]

Now Winters claims that "we are determined by history only to the extent that we fail to understand it."[10] In other words, a complete understanding of history would make us completely independent of it. This is absurd: however perfect our understanding, historical events have happened, and we find ourselves in the twentieth century in a different historical situation from those who lived in the sixteenth. We know four hundred years more of history than they, and the race has four hundred years more of experience to its credit. As our situation has changed, so must our outlook, to take some account of the change. This seems obvious, but I believe Winters would certainly hold that sensibility does *not* necessarily alter, or, if it does, needs no correspondingly altered expression to render it. The poet is not to be the mouthpiece of his age in any way. Yet it appears to be a matter of common experience for a large number of people that Bridges is archaic in the bad sense, out of key not only with his time but with what would be his own feelings if he knew them. Winters would doubtless make a characteristically ferocious retort: who am I to know what Bridges' feelings were like? how do I know that his verse wasn't perfectly in accord with them? But this is the point: we don't know because the poetry doesn't tell us.

For a more precise reply to Winters' charges it must be said, I think, that the second reason given ("social conditions") must be rejected for Winters' own reasons; but that the other cannot so lightly be dismissed. The sneer in inverted commas ("the stylistic advances of Eliot and Pound") represents a complete misconception.[11] As the quotation from Eliot makes clear, both words are misplaced. Much more than a *stylistic* change has happened, and it is offered not as an advance but as a change rendered necessary by a change in sensibility. It isn't to be argued that Eliot's manner of writing is better (or "more advanced") than Greville's or Marvell's or Johnson's or Wordsworth's—it is simply a manner relevant to the sensibility that belongs to Eliot, as a man alive in his own time. If a poet writes to communicate "a sound attitude to a major problem," he must know what a major problem is, which means having a particular perception of it. This perception, conditioned to a large degree by history, does not guarantee the quality of the expression, but it can hardly be communicated in a technique alien to the sensibility from which the perception issues.

Introduction

1. T. S. Eliot, "The Function of Criticism," *Selected Essays* (New York, 1950), pp. 13–14.

1 — *The Possibility of Relevance*

1. Harold Osborne, *Aesthetics and Criticism* (London, 1955), p. 170.

2. Perhaps he need not be *too* consistent. Cf. D. H. Lawrence in his essay on Galsworthy: "a good critic should give his reader a few standards to go by. He can change the standards for every new critical attempt, so long as he keeps good faith. But it is just as well to say: This and this is the standard we judge by."—"John Galsworthy," *Phoenix* (London, 1936), p. 539.

3. John Crowe Ransom, *The World's Body* (New York, 1938), p. 173.

4. *Ibid.*, p. 342.

5. *Aesthetics and Criticism*, p. 17 n.

6. *The World's Body*, pp. 330–31.

7. *Ibid.*, p. 329.

8. John Crowe Ransom, *The New Criticism* (Norfolk, Conn., 1941), p. xi.

9. *The World's Body*, p. 332.

10. *Ibid.*, p. 343.

11. John Crowe Ransom, "Criticism as Pure Speculation," *The Intent of the Critic* ed. by Donald A. Stauffer (Princeton, N. J., 1941), p. 94.

12. *The World's Body*, pp. 346–47. It is worth remembering that "prose" for Ransom usually means scientific

discourse. A gloss on the passage quoted reveals that "poetry differs from prose on the technical side by the devices which are, precisely its means of escaping from prose." That is to say, poetry is different from prose in just those ways in which it is different from prose.

13. At one point Ransom specifically refers to "aesthetic forms" as artificial, unconnected with the society in which they arise (see *The World's Body*, p. 39). However, in the essay "Poets Without Laurels" in the same book, he argues that to change the ways of poetry you must first change the ways of society. Inconsistencies of this kind are fairly common and presumably derive from the author's not asking what either generality means.

14. John Crowe Ransom, *God Without Thunder* (London, 1931), p. 197.

15. *The World's Body*, p. 31.

16. *The New Criticism*, p. 280.

17. *The Intent of the Critic*, p. 111.

18. *Ibid.*, pp. 107–8, 111.

19. *The World's Body*, p. 47. Strangely enough, Ransom (as literary critic) has quite a lot to say about Shakespeare's faulty structures and evidently thinks that these reduce his poetic merits. Of course, this may be a new use of the word. See *ibid.*, p. 278. I daresay it may be true of Milton that his subjects are treated more precisely in his tracts than in his verse. If so, it seems to me a severe comment on the success of his poetry—which is far from what Ransom intends. Cf. F. R. Leavis, *The Common Pursuit* (London, 1952), p. 124: "What Mr. Santayana calls 'Shakespeare's medium' creates what it conveys; 'previously definite' ideas put into a 'clear and transparent' medium wouldn't have been definite enough for Shakespeare's purpose." And we may remember Arnold on the subject of greatness in poetry.

20. *The New Criticism*, pp. 43–44.

21. *Ibid.*, pp. 218–20.

22. *The Intent of the Critic*, p. 107; my italics.

23. *Ibid.*, p. 112; my italics.

24. *The New Criticism*, p. 54.

25. *The World's Body*, p. 219.

26. Edward Bullough, *Aesthetics: Lectures & Essays* ed. by Elizabeth M. Wilkinson (Stanford, Cal., 1957), p. 66.

27. At times Ransom plays with the idea of poetry as a special kind of knowledge: "The true poetry has no great interest in improving or idealizing the world, which does well enough. It only wants to realize the world, to see it better. Poetry is the kind of knowledge by which we must know what we have arranged that we shall not know otherwise."—*The World's Body*, p. x. *Who* has arranged? But hints thrown out like this are so vague and unconnected that it is impossible to follow them to any profitable conclusion.

28. *The World's Body*, pp. 57–58, 59.

29. Yvor Winters, *In Defense of Reason* (Denver, 1947), pp. 527–33.

30. *The World's Body*, p. 60.

31. *The New Criticism*, p. 208.

32. John Crowe Ransom, "Poetry: The Formal Analysis," *Kenyon Review*, IX (1947), 438.

33. *The World's Body*, p. 333.

34. *Ibid.*, p. 345.

35. *The Common Pursuit*, p. 241.

36. T. S. Eliot, "Religion and Literature," *Selected Essays* (New York, 1950), p. 343.

37. *Ibid.*, p. 353.

38. Vincent Buckley, *Poetry and Morality* (London, 1959), p. 219.

39. D. J. Enright cites an instance of just how different, when he quotes Walter Stein as stating "that the Christian critic's primary claim 'to a privileged perspective in the task of arriving at ultimate evaluations' lies in the fact that 'the standpoint of Christianity is the standpoint of truth.' "—*The Apothecary's Shop* (London, 1957), p. 27.

40. *The Common Pursuit*, p. 224.

41. T. S. Eliot, "Poetry and Drama," *On Poetry and Poets* (London, 1957), p. 87.

42. F. R. Leavis, *Revaluation* (London, 1936), p. 2.

43. *The Common Pursuit*, pp. 160–72.

44. *Ibid.*, p. 167.

45. *Ibid.*, p. 166.

46. *Ibid.*, p. 114.

47. Yvor Winters, *The Function of Criticism* (Denver, 1957), p. 26.

48. F. R. Leavis, *The Great Tradition* (New York, n.d.), pp. 30, 112, 56.

49. *In Defense of Reason*, p. 6.

50. *The Common Pursuit*, p. 89.

51. *In Defense of Reason*, p. 29.

2 — Strategic Selection: Criticism by Choice of Terms

1. Kenneth Burke, *The Philosophy of Literary Form* (New York, 1957) p. ix.

2. Christopher Caudwell, *Illusion and Reality* (London, 1937), pp. 20-21.

3. "Marxist critics . . . are not only students of literature and society but prophets of the future, monitors, propagandists; and they have difficulty in keeping these two functions separate."—René Wellek and Austin Warren, *Theory of Literature* (New York, 1949), pp. 89-90.

4. Marius Bewley, "Kenneth Burke as Literary Critic," *Scrutiny*, XV (Dec. 1948), 258.

5. *The Philosophy of Literary Form*, pp. 139-40.

6. *Ibid.*, p. 141.

7. Cf. Kenneth Burke, *Permanence & Change*, 2nd rev. ed. (Los Altos, Cal., 1954), p. 77: "Refined critics, of the Matthew Arnold variety, assumed that exquisiteness of taste was restricted to the 'better' classes of people, those who never had names ending in 'ug.' Yet if we can bring ourselves to imagine Matthew Arnold loafing on the corner with the gashouse gang, we promptly realize how undiscriminating he would prove himself. Everything about him would be inappropriate: both what he said and the ways in which he said it. Consider the crudeness of his perception as regards the proper oaths, the correct way of commenting upon passing women, the etiquette of spitting. Does not his very crassness here

reveal the presence of a morality, a deeply felt and piously obeyed sense of the appropriate, on the part of these men, whose linkages he would outrageously violate? Watch them—and observe with what earnestness, what *devotion*, these gashouse Matthew Arnolds act to prove themselves, every minute of the day, true members of their cult. Vulgarity is pious."

I wonder how much Burke knows of the proper oaths, etc. Possibly his use of "piety" here is just about legitimate. But it is so extended that his manner of slipping from "piety" to "morality" and back again is inexcusable. Arnold's "crassness" does not reveal a morality, only an expertise. And vulgarity, if pious, is not moral. The clever placing of "proper," "correct," "appropriate," and "etiquette" (a borderline case but the moral tone seems intentional) seems designed to prejudge the issue the other way. The propriety and correctness may be exquisite, but how do they relate to taste? If there is a piety linking the practices of vulgarity, it is not one that guarantees even their interest away from the gashouse. Burke seems to suggest that this is not something we should make judgments upon. I think we should; but we should also make sure that we know our opponent first, and have hold of something more than a dummy which we have dressed up with his name.

8. *The Philosophy of Literary Form*, pp. 164–89.

9. Lionel Trilling, *The Liberal Imagination* (New York, 1950), pp. 223–42.

10. *The Philosophy of Literary Form*, p. 142.

11. Quoted by Bewley, who comments: "Here one can see how easily, without an exacting critical conscience, Burke's theory moves through art to propaganda. . . . It is not merely that one may not like what Burke is propagandizing. . . . it is not that one wholly disagrees with the idea of art *as propaganda*, but the cold-blooded sacrifice of art *to* propaganda that is implicit here is repellent."—*Scrutiny*, XV (Dec. 1948), 260.

12. Burke's establishment of Marxist criticism appears innocently simple: "Marxist criticism in recent years

'triumphed' over its most emphatic opponents. Even those critics who had previously been answering questions about 'pure form' now began answering questions about 'the relation between art and society,' i.e. *Marxist* questions." —*The Philosophy of Literary Form*, p. 57. But the Marxist approach involves always the dogma of the priority of economic conditions—which makes Burke's statement disingenuous.

13. *The Philosophy of Literary Form*, p. 262.

14. *Permanence & Change*, p. 66.

15. Kenneth Burke, *Counter-Statement*, 2nd ed. (Los Altos, Cal., 1953), pp. 184–85.

16. *Ibid.*, p. 113.

17. *Ibid.*, pp. x, xv.

18. *Ibid.*, pp. 76–77.

19. *The Philosophy of Literary Form*, p. 75.

20. See Appendix A for a detailed discussion of one of Burke's expositions.

21. *The Philosophy of Literary Form*, p. 57.

22. *Ibid.*, p. 3.

23. *Ibid.*, p. 261.

24. *Ibid.*

25. Later Burke replaces his situation-strategy pair by a group of five terms: act, scene, agent, agency, purpose (*Ibid.*, p. 90, n. 6). This scheme has the possible virtue of greater complexity (a virtue if it relates more closely to its subject-matter, a nuisance if it does not); but I cannot see that otherwise it meets the objections that I bring against Burke's earlier formula. Also the explicit invocations of "purpose" makes for a dangerous kind of over-simplification, as I have remarked above.

26. *Ibid.*, p. 260.

27. Cf. *Ibid.*, pp. 54, 42.

28. *Ibid.*, p. 257.

29. *Ibid.*, pp. 260–61.

30. *Ibid.*, p. 259.

31. Quoted by L. C. Knights in his review of Elmer Edgar Stoll's book *Art and Artifice in Shakespeare*, *Scrutiny*, III (June 1934), 88.

32. Some of the incidental remarks in this piece are rather tiresome: Brutus "is virtuous because he does for Romans what you want your popular leaders to do for you. He takes on the nobility that comes of being good for private enterprise." — *The Philosophy of Literary Form*, p. 283. A second Shakesperian monologue, "Trial Translation (from *Twelfth Night*)," is a good deal less interesting and in parts notably obscure.

33. *Ibid.*, p. 256.

34. *Ibid.*

35. *Ibid.*, p. 261.

3 — The Rationalist Ideal

1. Yvor Winters, *The Function of Criticism* (Denver, 1957), p. 15.

2. For example, William Barrett, "Temptations of St. Yvor," *Kenyon Review*, IX (Autumn 1947), 532–51. The temptation of moral absolutism is the one he thinks Winters should have been especially careful to avoid.

3. Yvor Winters, *In Defense of Reason* (Denver, 1947), p. 361; my italics.

4. *Ibid.*, p. 11.

5. *Ibid.*, p. 10.

6. *Ibid.*, p. 76. Winters no longer appears to share the unanimity with regard to Homer: "My ignorance of Greek prevents my forming an opinion of individual passages in Homer, though I am willing to believe that there are many which are great; but the total action and the details of the action are simply incapable of resulting in a great work." — *The Function of Criticism*, p. 42.

7. *The Function of Criticism*, p. 17.

8. *In Defense of Reason*, p. 3.

9. *The Function of Criticism*, p. 17.

10. *Ibid.*, p. 103. Theory — that is to say, consciously enunciated principles — plays an important part for Winters in the writing of poetry also. So, "If he [the poet] has real poetic talent, reasonable scholarship, and the power of generalization, this interest [in the work of other

poets] may lead to the formulation of valid critical principles, more or less general and inclusive, depending on his
intellectual powers. These principles may in turn free him
from the tyranny of historical fashions . . . , may aid him
to choose sounder themes and sounder methods of structure, and by virtue of these to achieve greater precision of
detail."—*Ibid.*, p. 22. Theory in the critic may have other
effects, as when Winters compares three poems by Donne,
Bridges, and Hopkins "with reference to a particular
theory of poetry. The poems by Donne and Bridges con-
form to this theory and illustrate it perfectly; the poem by
Hopkins deviates sharply and I believe suffers as a result."
—*Ibid.*, p. 103.

11. *In Defense of Reason*, p. 372.
12. *Ibid.*, p. 20.
13. *Ibid.*, p. 31; my italics.
14. *Ibid.*, p. 363.
15. *Ibid.*, p. 11.
16. *The Function of Criticism*, p. 26.
17. *In Defense of Reason*, p. 367.
18. *Ibid.*, p. 491.
19. *Ibid.*, pp. 57–58.
20. *Ibid.*, p. 57, n. 32.
21. *Ibid.*, p. 58, n. 32.
22. *Ibid.*, p. 365.
23. Such a determinist view sorts well with Burke's
political views and is a main object of attack in Winters'
criticism.
24. John Crowe Ransom, *The New Criticism* (Norfolk,
Conn., 1941), pp. 20–21.
25. *In Defense of Reason*, p. 367. How precise the adjustment is to be is well illustrated by the following passage: "Miss Rowena Lockett once remarked to me that
Laforgue resembles a person who speaks with undue harsh-
ness and then apologizes; whereas he should have made
the necessary subtractions before speaking. The objection
implies an attitude more sceptical and cautious than that
of Mr. Burke; instead of irony as the remedy for the
unsatisfactory feeling, it recommends the waste-basket and

a new beginning. And this recommendation has its basis not only in morality but in aesthetics: the romantic ironists . . . write imperfectly in proportion to their irony; their attitude, which is a corruption of feeling, entails a corruption of style—that is, the irony is an admission of careless feeling, which is to say careless writing, and the stylist is weak in proportion to the grounds for his irony." —*Ibid.*, pp. 72–73.

26. So can "attitude," I suppose; but it seems more natural to talk of the right attitude to take up in a given situation than of the right feeling to have.

27. *In Defense of Reason*, p. 150.

28. *The Function of Criticism*, p. 51.

29. Cf. *In Defense of Reason*, p. 19: "verse is more valuable than prose . . . for the simple reasons that its rhythms are faster and more highly organized than those of prose, and so lend themselves to a greater complexity and compression of relationship, and that the intensity of this convention renders possible a greater intensity of other desirable conventions, such as poetic language and devices of rhetoric. The writer of prose must substitute bulk for this kind of intensity; he must define his experience ordinarily by giving all of its past history, the narrative logic leading up to it, whereas the experiental relations given in a good lyric poem, though particular in themselves, are applicable without alteration to a good many past histories. In this sense, the lyric is general as well as particular."

30. *Ibid.*, p. 219.

31. *Ibid.*, p. 72.

32. Originally published in two parts in *The Hudson Review* (Winter, 1949 and Spring, 1949); reprinted in *The Function of Criticism*.

33. *The Function of Criticism*, p. 126.

34. *Ibid.*, p. 133.

35. *Ibid.*, p. 134.

36. "The bird has the advantage merely of the Romantic and sentimental feeling attached to birds as symbols of the free and unrestrained spirit, a feeling derived

very largely from Shelley's *Skylark* and from a handful of similar—and similarly bad—poems of the past century and a half."—*Ibid.*, pp. 133–34.

37. *Ibid.*, p. 124.

38. It is worth remarking that for Winters Shakespeare's sonnets (not any of the plays) represent, "I suppose, our standard of the greatest possible poetry." So it is presumably this particular Renaissance poet whose methods are implicitly invoked. Hopkins does, I think, often develop concepts and occasionally in something like a Renaissance manner (for example: *As kingfishers catch fire*, where the concept embodied in the imagery at the start is followed through and enlarged to the end of the poem).

39. *The Function of Criticism*, p. 125.

40. *Ibid.*, p. 90.

41. *Ibid.*, p. 142.

42. *In Defense of Reason*, pp. 17–18.

43. *Ibid.*, p. 23. Elsewhere "form" has a rather more casually applied meaning. Of W. C. Williams we learn that "Such poems as *The Widow's Lament* or *To Waken an Old Lady* are fully realized; the form is complete and perfect; the feeling is sound. Dr. Williams has a surer feeling for language than any other poet of his generation, save, perhaps, Stevens at his best. But he is wholly incapable of coherent thought."—*Ibid.*, p. 93. So Dr. Williams writes poems whose form is perfect and complete without being able to think—in the absence, that is to say, of just that which Winters (rightly) holds form to characterize.

44. *The Function of Criticism*, p. 22.

45. *In Defense of Reason*, p. 64, n. 37.

46. *Ibid.*, p. 144.

47. *Ibid.*, p. 61.

48. *Ibid.*, p. 497. "The subject matter of *The Waste Land* is in general similar to that of *Les Fleurs du Mal*. Yet if one will compare let us say *Le Jeu* with *A Game of Chess*, one may perhaps note what Eliot overlooked. Eliot, in dealing with debased and stupid material, felt himself obliged to seek his form in his matter: the result is con-

fusion and journalistic reproduction of detail. Baudelaire, in dealing with similar matter, sought to evaluate it in terms of eternal verity: he sought his form and his point of view in tradition, and from that point of view and in that form he judged his material, and the result is a profound evaluation of evil. The difference is the difference between triviality and greatness." —*Ibid.*, p. 499.

It is tempting to see Winters' preference—and even his conception of "tradition"—as lying in something as relatively subordinate as Baudelaire's regular stanza and meter, the one thing he has in common with Bridges. Otherwise it is hard to understand in what way Baudelaire sought his "point of view" in tradition. Interestingly enough, *Le Jeu* goes near to an explicit comment only in the final stanza: the poem is a very fine one, but, if it has a fault, it is surely in that phrase *l'abîme béant*. Elsewhere the poem avoids direct expression of its author's position vis-à-vis his material; yet we have no difficulty in assessing it.

For Winters on Eliot see, further, Appendix B.

49. *The Function of Criticism*, p. 186. Cf. "Stevens is released from all the restraints of Christianity, and is encouraged by all the modern orthodoxy of Romanticism: his hedonism is so fused with Romanticism as to be merely an elegant variation on that somewhat inelegant System of Thoughtlessness. His ideas have remained essentially unchanged for more than a quarter of a century, and on the whole they have been very clearly expressed; so that there is no real occasion to be in doubt as to their nature; and he began as a great poet, so that when we examine the effect of those ideas upon his work, we are examining something of very great importance." —*In Defense of Reason*, p. 459.

50. Another instance closely bearing on this issue is his extraordinarily imperceptive dismissal of Pope's *Elegy to the Memory of an Unfortunate Lady*: he refers merely to its "genteel ineptitude." —*In Defense of Reason*, p. 136. Cf. Leavis' account in *Revaluation* (London, 1936), pp. 69–76.

51. *In Defense of Reason*, pp. 82–83.

52. Winters appears to have had something of a change of heart (or mind) over Milton, for in 1956 he exclaimed: "It requires more than a willing suspension of disbelief to read most of Milton; it requires a willing suspension of intelligence."—*The Function of Criticism*, p. 43.

53. *In Defense of Reason*, p. 491.

54. *Ibid.*

55. Ransom, on the other hand, thinks that an "imitation" must be *better* than its original—"in one thing only: not being actual, it cannot be used, it can only be known." —*The World's Body* (New York, 1938), pp. 196–97.

56. *The Function of Criticism*, p. 57.

57. Elsewhere Winters remarks on the "almost insoluble problem" of a dramatist "imitating the speech of a character of moderate intelligence in a situation of which the character does not in any serious sense understand the meaning."—*Ibid.*, p. 52. But, for example, there is a speech by Cominius (*Coriolanus*, Act II, scene 2, line 80 ff.) in which Shakespeare's penetrating moral comment is achieved *through* the very insensitivity of the speaker. (See the article by D. A. Traversi in *Scrutiny*, VI (June 1937), especially 49–52.) Winters is always hampered in his (rather rare) discussions of drama by taking the mimetic principle very solemnly indeed, and by talking always in terms of "character": "A novelist would be able to write *about* Macbeth and his state of mind, and would thus have an advantage over the dramatist, who must exhibit Macbeth's state of mind in words *in some sense appropriate* to Macbeth in that state of mind. The novelist could employ the best prose of which he might be capable; the poet cannot employ the best poetry of which he is capable, for such poetry would be out of character—such poetry has to wait until later, when Macbeth has been educated up to the point at which he can speak it plausibly."—*The Function of Criticism*, p. 53; my italics. Winters seems to be as far away from Shakespeare's characteristic mastery of language as Johnson; he makes the point, reasonable enough when one considers only an

isolated passage, that the dagger speech is not very good poetry, but puts this down to the causes suggested in this quotation. If Macbeth hasn't been educated up to the point where great poetry is possible by this stage, the great speech in Act I, scene 7 seems unaccountable. I should say that the speech of Cominius referred to above *is* great poetry, though of a rather unusual kind which cannot be appreciated outside its position in the drama.

58. *In Defense of Reason*, p. 240.

59. *Ibid.*, p. 247.

4—The Limits of Relevance

1. F. R. Leavis, *The Common Pursuit* (London, 1952), pp. 110–11.

2. *Ibid.*, p. 110.

3. F. R. Leavis, "Reality and Sincerity," *Scrutiny*, XIX (Winter 1952–53), 90–98.

4. *Ibid.*, 92–93.

5. *Ibid.*, p. 96.

6. Vincent Buckley, *Poetry and Morality* (London, 1959), p. 171.

7. Leavis' treatment of Emily Brontë's poem seems to me rather less satisfactory than that of Hardy's and rather more inclined to take the will for the deed.

8. F. R. Leavis, " 'Thought' and Emotional Quality," *Scrutiny*, XIII (Spring 1945), 59.

9. *The Common Pursuit*, p. 20.

10. F. R. Leavis, *The Great Tradition* (New York, n.d.), pp. 91–93. To some extent Henry James's criticism provides the model for this of Leavis. For instance: "Emma Bovary, in spite of the nature of her consciousness and in spite of her reflecting so much that of her creator, is really too small an affair. . . . Why did Flaubert choose, as special conduits of the life he proposed to depict, such inferior and in the case of Frédéric such abject human specimens? I insist only in respect to the latter, the perfection of *Madame Bovary* scarce leaving one much warrant for wishing anything other. Even here, however, the

general scale and size of Emma, who is small even of her sort, should be a warning to hyperbole. If I say that in the matter of Frédéric at all events the answer is inevitably detrimental I mean that it weighs heavily on our author's general credit. He wished in each case to make a picture of experience—middling experience, it is true—and of the world close to him; but if he imagined nothing better for his purpose than such a heroine and such a hero, both such limited reflectors and registers, we are forced to believe it to have been by a defect of his mind. And that sign of weakness remains even if it be objected that the images in question were addressed to his purpose better than others would have been: the purpose itself then shows as inferior."—Henry James, *Notes on Novelists* (New York, 1914). See *Selected Literary Criticism* ed. Morris Shapira (London, 1963), pp. 222–23. The characteristically trenchant tone to which this passage owes much of its convincingness is James's own and comes doubtless from his own standpoint as a novelist. Leavis' tone is almost always more exploratory, but the seriousness and forthrightness in each come from a common conception of criticism.

11. *The Common Pursuit*, p. 228.

12. Harold Osborne, *Aesthetics and Criticism* (London, 1955), pp. 67–68.

13. Cf. Joseph Wood Krutch's observation of Johnson's criticism: "Its manner is objective, and its aim is not to present 'the truth as I (and probably no one else) see it,' but to make statements which the reader will accept as true for himself and for all normal men."—*Samuel Johnson* (New York, 1944), p. 497.

14. *The Great Tradition*, p. 8.

15. *The Common Pursuit*, p. 226. On this particular issue, cf. Yvor Winters, *In Defense of Reason* (Denver, 1947), pp. 308–9.

16. F. R. Leavis, "Mr. Pryce-Jones, the British Council and British Culture," *Scrutiny*, XVIII (Winter 1951–52), 227.

17. *Scrutiny*, II (March 1934), 332.

18. Eric Bentley, ed., *The Importance of Scrutiny* (New York, 1948), p. 395.

19. F. R. Leavis, "The Responsible Critic," *Scrutiny*, XIX (Spring 1953), 178–79.

20. F. R. Leavis, "What's Wrong with Criticism?" *Scrutiny*, I (Sept., 1932), 145–46.

21. Lionel Trilling, *A Gathering of Fugitives* (London, 1957), p. 105.

22. Lionel Trilling, *The Liberal Imagination* (New York, 1950), p. 9.

23. *Ibid.*, p. 259.

24. F. R. Leavis, " 'The Literary Mind,' " *Scrutiny*, I (May 1932), 30–31.

25. F. R. Leavis & Denys Thompson, *Culture and Environment* (London, 1950), pp. 1–2. Also, *ibid.*, pp. 2–3: "And the cultivation of the art of speech was as essential to the old popular culture that in local variations existed throughout the country as song, dance and handicrafts. Other things that may have been essential a study of *Pilgrim's Progress*, the supreme expression of the old English people, will perhaps suggest. At any rate, this great book, which is so much more than Bunyan's, will, together with (say) *Change in the Village*, *The Wheelwright's Shop*, and the other works of George 'Bourne' (or Sturt), and, for an account of the process of dissolution, *Middletown*, serve to bring home to the doubting that the English people did once have a culture (so nearly forgotten now that the educated often find it hard to grasp what the assertion means)."

26. Raymond Williams, *Culture and Society* (New York, 1958), p. 259.

27. On this aspect of folk-cultures, see Albert B. Lord, *The Singer of Tales* (Cambridge, Mass., 1960). Writing mainly of the tradition of oral epic poetry in Yugoslavia, Lord demonstrates convincingly how it is being killed by increasing literacy. The skills involved in learning to sing long traditional epics were beyond question unconsciously acquired: in almost no case was a singer able to give a coherent account of how he learnt his art—and this not

through any lack of intelligence or through being unused to verbal expression.

28. F. R. Leavis, "Restatements for Critics," *Scrutiny*, I (March 1933), 316.

29. Max Beloff, *Europe and the Europeans: An International Discussion* (London, 1957), p. 111.

30. F. R. Leavis, *Revaluation* (London, 1936), pp. 178–79.

31. *Ibid.*, pp. 170–71.

32. *Ibid.*, p. 165.

33. *The Great Tradition*, p. 163.

34. D. H. Lawrence, *The Rainbow*, Chap. I.

35. F. R. Leavis, *D. H. Lawrence: Novelist* (New York, 1955), p. 111.

36. *The Common Pursuit*, p. 130.

37. *Ibid.*, p. 132.

38. *In Defense of Reason*, p. 14.

39. Winters' attitude is "*universalia ante rem*" with a vengeance; but it is difficult to attach much meaning to his word "located," for the physical meaning is impossible, and any metaphorical one stretched too far even for such elusive things as truths. Oddly enough Barrett, in the article referred to above (see Chapter 3, note 2), takes Winters' argument at its face value, and as if to pour scorn on him, asks where he thought the truths were located before he came to his theism.

40. *D. H. Lawrence: Novelist*, p. 75.

41. Cf. "Literature and Society," *The Common Pursuit*, especially pp. 189–90, where Leavis discusses the background of Bunyan's art: "we have the idiomatic life that runs to saw and proverb, and runs also to what is closely akin to these, the kind of pungently characterizing epitome represented by 'turncoat.' . . . The vitality here is not merely one of raciness; an art of civilized living is implicit, with its habits and standards of serious moral valuation."

42. Cf. the end of Leavis' essay on Bunyan: "*The Pilgrim's Progress* must leave us asking whether without something corresponding to what is supremely affirmed in

that exaltation [of the book's close], without an equivalently sanctioned attitude to death that is at the same time a 'stimulus to further living' . . . , there can be such a thing as cultural health."—*The Common Pursuit*, p. 210.

43. F. R. Leavis, "Restatements for Critics," *Scrutiny*, I (March 1933), 316.

APPENDIX A—*Burke's Method in Action*

1. *Accent*, Autumn, 1943. Reprinted in Stanley Edgar Hyman's anthology, *The Critical Performance* (New York, 1956).

2. Stanley Edgar Hyman, *The Critical Performance*, p. 259.

3. *Ibid.*, pp. 275–76.

4. *Ibid.*, p. 264.

5. *Ibid.*, p. 266.

6. Forever *warm* too—which as the Cold Pastoral of the last stanza testifies, is just what it isn't.

7. Stanley Edgar Hyman, *The Critical Performance*, p. 265. Cf. *ibid.*, p. 262; "The Ode is striving to move beyond the region of becoming into the realm of *being*. (This is another way of saying that we are here concerned with two levels of motivation.)"

8. *Ibid.*, p. 261.

9. *Ibid.*, p. 269.

10. *Ibid.*, p. 276.

APPENDIX B—*Winters and Eliot*

1. Vincent Buckley, *Poetry and Morality* (London, 1959), p. 96.

2. T. S. Eliot, "The Function of Criticism," *Selected Essays* (New York, 1950), p. 19.

3. *Poetry and Morality*, p. 106.

4. Yvor Winters, *In Defense of Reason* (Denver, 1947), pp. 489–90.

5. *Ibid.*, pp. 491–92.

6. *Ibid.*, p. 483.

7. *Ibid.*, pp. 498-99.

8. *Ibid.*, p. 101.

9. T. S. Eliot, "Poetry in the Eighteenth Century," *The Pelican Guide to English Literature* ed. by Boris Ford (Harmondsworth, 1957), IV, pp. 271-72.

10. Yvor Winters, *The Function of Criticism* (Denver, 1957), p. 22.

11. Some criticism may seem to give lodgment for Winters' comment. Q. D. Leavis in a review writes, "Mr. Morgan (and the other novelists of this kind) for all their earnest determination to be literary might not be writing in an age that has witnessed the innovations of Joyce, Proust, Lawrence and Mrs. Woolf."—*Scrutiny*, I (Sept. 1932), 180-81. The formulation is unfortunate, but the previous sentence suggests that the "innovations" represent a technique through which these writers have rediscovered in our time their own emotional roots.

INDEX

"Aesthetic" as critical term: Ransom's use of, 21; Bullough's use of, 21–22; Leavis objects to, 36

Aesthetic attitudes, 115–16

Anderson, Quentin, 117

Arnold, Matthew: compared to Burke, 42; Burke's travesty of, 156n7; mentioned, 7, 27, 37, 120–21, 154n19

Austen, Jane: *Emma*, 116

Autonomy of art: Ransom's views on, 9, 11. *See also* Intrinsic value

Barrett, William: criticizes Winters, 159n2, 168n39

Baudelaire, Charles: *Le Jeu*, 162n48; mentioned, 93

Beloff, Max: *Europe and the Europeans*, 127–29

Bewley, Marius: on Marxist criticism, 40; on Burke, 157n11

Blackmur, Richard: on Burke's method, 56

Bridges, Robert: *Low Barometer*, 88–89; Winters' view of, 88–89, 151–52, 160n10; mentioned, 91, 152

Brontë, Emily, 102–4

Buckley, Vincent: on Christian criticism, 30–31; criticizes Leavis, 106–8; on Winters and Eliot, 145–46; mentioned, 136

—*Poetry and Morality*, 106–7, 145–46

Bullough, Edward: *Aesthetics*, 21–22

Bunyan, John: Leavis on, 167n25, 168n41, 169n42

Burke, Kenneth: his Marxist approach to art, xiii, 44–50, 158n12; on nature of literature, 39, 49, 50–54; pragmatism, 40, 53–54; on style, 41–42; compared to Arnold, 42; on perception, 43–44; critical vocabulary, 46–49, 55–56, 158n25; on situation and strategy, 48–49, 55–65 *passim*, 158n25; his method analyzed, 56–65, 139–44; on proverbs, 63–64; on Keats, 139–144; travesty of Arnold, 156n7; mentioned, 18, 66, 80, 160n23, 160n25

—"Antony in Behalf of the Play," 62–63; *Attitudes Toward History*, 44–46; *Counterstatement*, 48, 50–53 *passim*; "The Logic of Hitler's Battle," 43, 45; *Permanence and Change*,